JOURNEY
to the
KINGDOM

An Insider's Look at the
Liturgy and Beliefs
of the
Eastern
Orthodox Church

Fr. Vassilios Papavassiliou

PARACLETE PRESS
BREWSTER, MASSACHUSETTS

Journey to the Kingdom: An Insider's Look at the Liturgy and Beliefs of the Eastern Orthodox Church

2018 Second Printing
2012 First Printing

ISBN 978-1-61261-164-8

Scriptures marked (NIrV) are taken from the Holy Bible, NEW INTERNATIONAL READER'S VERSION®. Copyright © 1996, 1998 Biblica. All rights reserved throughout the world. Used by permission of Biblica.

Scriptures marked (NIV) are taken from the Holy Bible, NEW INTERNATIONAL VERSION®, NIV® Copyright © 1973, 1978, 1984, 2011 by Biblica, Inc.™ Used by permission. All rights reserved worldwide.

Scriptures marked (ESV) are taken from The Holy Bible, English Standard Version® (ESV®), copyright © 2001 by Crossway, a publishing ministry of Good News Publishers. Used by permission. All rights reserved.

Scriptures marked (NKJV) are taken from the New King James Version. Copyright © 1982 by Thomas Nelson, Inc. Used by permission. All rights reserved.

Scriptures marked (EL) were translated by Fr. Ephrem Lash.

Scriptures marked (VP) are the author's own translations.

The Paraclete Press name and logo (dove on cross) are trademarks of Paraclete Press, Inc.

Library of Congress Cataloging-in-Publication Data

Papavassiliou, Vassilios.
  Journey to the kingdom : an insider's look at the liturgy and beliefs of the Eastern Orthodox church / Fr. Vassilios Papavassiliou.
     p. cm.
  Includes bibliographical references.
  ISBN 978-1-61261-164-8 (trade pbk.)
  1. Orthodox Eastern Church—Doctrines. 2. Lord's Supper—Orthodox Eastern Church. 3. Lord's Supper (Liturgy) 4. Orthodox Eastern Church—Liturgy. I. Title.
  BX323.P37 2012
  264'.019--dc23   2012019328

    10 9 8 7 6 5 4 3

Published by Paraclete Press
Brewster, Massachusetts
www.paracletepress.com
Printed in the United States of America

Contents

JOURNEY
to the
KINGDOM

1. *Church interior and icon screen*

Come In And See

Come, I will show you the bride, the wife of the Lamb.
—Rev. 21:9, NRIV

This is your invitation to come in and see
how Orthodox Christians all over the world
worship. Perhaps you have heard something
about what we call the Divine Liturgy, the beauty of
its expressions, the profundity with which this special
service offers its participants a way to encounter God?
If so, this book will take your understanding to the
next level.

How better to get to know a faith than by
experiencing, albeit secondhand, its primary form of
worship? The sights and the symbols. The words of
faith and the mysteries that are plumbed. Through
twenty brief chapters, and just as many black-and-white
photographs, you will learn much more.

In many ways, this book could be regarded as a form
of liturgical catechism, or instruction about worship,
for any and all interested in joining the Orthodox

Church. But it is also more than that, as I hope that anyone—whether Orthodox already, considering joining an Orthodox church, or the simply curious—will find this tour of our liturgy and worship helpful and inspiring.

Journey to the Kingdom is not a work of scholarship. It is not a formal study of worship or liturgical history, nor is it a comprehensive commentary on the Divine Liturgy of the Orthodox Church. The purpose of this book is to explain the meaning of our worship, what happens at the service of the Divine Liturgy throughout the world, and the part that every Orthodox Christian plays in it.

By "Eastern Orthodox Church" we mean the family of Christian churches that traces its origins to Jesus Christ, acknowledges the authority of seven Ecumenical Councils, and is in communion with the ancient patriarchates of Constantinople, Alexandria, Antioch, and Jerusalem. These churches are defined by a strong sense not of being a denomination but of the continuing Christian Church that emerged in Jerusalem some two thousand years ago, as well as their adherence—despite their varied origins, liturgical practices, and customs—to what we refer to as the Byzantine rite.

The "standard" Liturgy in all Eastern Orthodox Churches is that of St. John Chrysostom (ca. 347–407, archbishop of Constantinople). The Liturgy of St. Basil the Great (ca. 330–379, archbishop of Caesarea) is celebrated usually ten times a year: on the five Sundays of Great Lent, Christmas Eve, the Eve of Theophany, Great Thursday, Great Saturday, and on his feast day (January 1). Many of the prayers of the clergy in St. Basil's Liturgy are different and considerably longer than those of St. John's Liturgy.

On the weekdays of Great Lent (the forty-day period before Holy Week; Holy Week is when we celebrate the Passion and Resurrection of Christ), normal liturgies are not celebrated, except on the great feast of the Annunciation (March 25). Because liturgies are always a celebration, they are deemed inappropriate in Lent except on days on which we celebrate the Resurrection (Saturdays and Sundays) or a great feast like the Annunciation. In order that Christians may receive Communion more frequently during the period of Lent, we have the Liturgy of the Presanctified Gifts on Wednesdays and Fridays. This is a more somber service than other liturgies. It is called the Liturgy of the Presanctified Gifts because there is no consecration of the bread and wine. Instead, a portion of the Eucharist from the Sunday Liturgy is kept aside for these weekday services. Hence the term Presanctified Gifts, meaning that the holy gifts—that is, the bread and wine of the Eucharist—are from the very beginning of the service the Body and Blood of Christ, having been sanctified already at a previous Liturgy.

When Vladimir the Great (958–1015) sent envoys around the world to study different religions so that he could decide which one to embrace, they did not inquire about doctrines or moral rules. Instead they watched those various religions at prayer, and it was the Divine Liturgy that they attended at the Church of Hagia Sophia in Constantinople that won them over. The best introduction to Orthodox Christianity is its primary act of worship. Of course, this book is no substitute for the real thing—it serves only as a guide and informant to enrich and shed light on that experience. But the Liturgy is not just prayer and song—it is rich with theology. What follows, therefore, is not only a guide to the Liturgy but also an introduction to Orthodoxy *through* the Liturgy.

The Divine Liturgy

Antidoron
Dismissal
Prayer Behind the Ambo
Thanksgiving
Communion of
Clergy + People
The Lord's Prayer
Litany of the Lord's Prayer

Prayers of Remembrance
The Epiclesis
The Mystical (Last) Supper
Holy, Holy, Holy Lord Sabaoth
Let us stand with awe

THE HOLY OBLATION

THE CREED

The Liturgy of the Holy Gifts

Completion of Cherubic Hymn

Litany of the Precious Gifts

Entrance of the Holy Gifts

The Cherubic Hymn
(first half/Psalm 50)

Prayers of the Faithful

Prayers for + Dismissal of Catechumens
Litany of Fervent Supplication

Entrance of the Gospel

The Trisagion

Apolytikia + Kontakia
(main hymns of the day)

Epistle + Alleluaria

Gospel (+ Sermon)

Little Litany
The Mini Creed
Second Set of Antiphons
Little Litany
First Set of Antiphons

The Liturgy of the Word

THE ANTIPHONS

The Great Litany
The Blessing

PROSKOMIDI   MATINS

IC XC
NI KA

❖ 1 ❖

The Blessing and Litany of Peace

Come, you blessed of My Father,
inherit the kingdom prepared for you
from the foundation of the world.
—MATT. 25:34, NKJV

O ur Divine Liturgy can be understood as a journey, and before we begin any journey, we need to know where we are going. Thus the Liturgy begins[1] with the announcement of our destination: "Blessed is the Kingdom of the Father and of the Son and of the Holy Spirit, now and forever, and to the ages of ages."

It is true: our destination is none other than the Kingdom of God, the Kingdom of the Trinity. But our journey really begins the moment we leave the house. Without this sacrificial act of leaving the comfort of our beds and homes and coming to church, there can be no liturgy, and whether we have to travel many miles or just walk a few yards down the street, a sacrificial act of worship has already begun.

We come to church not simply to add a spiritual and religious dimension to our secular lives, nor simply to meet our fellow Christians and to socialize, but above all to *become* the Church, to become the Kingdom of God. The biblical word for Church, *ekklesia*, means "gathering," or "assembly," and for the early Christians, this is precisely what Church meant. We begin our participation in worship before we even arrive at the church—simply by making the decision to come. By all means, come!

The gathering at the Divine Liturgy is also what we refer to as Eucharistic. In other words, its purpose and fulfillment is to participate in the Eucharist, the most essential aspect of the Liturgy, in which the Lord's Supper is accomplished. This cannot happen, under normal circumstances, at home. And it is the most important kind of meal—in fact, the *only* kind of meal—Christians are instructed to eat together in church. In his first epistle to the Corinthians, St. Paul admonishes the Christians of Corinth for partaking of a meal other than the Eucharist while they were gathered together (1 Cor. 11:20–22).

There are many reasons to come to Church, but there is only one good reason: to meet Christ—to pray, to be in the presence of God, and to worship Him. This is the unique, incredible opportunity that we have with the Eucharist, and this is how and why the social life and every other activity of the Church flows from the Liturgy. We gather together to reveal the true nature of the Church—to become what we are: the Body of Christ. The Liturgy reveals the Kingdom of God because in it Christ Himself becomes physically present in the Eucharist. Thus we gather together to become what we refer to as the Eucharistic assembly.

Blessed Is the Kingdom

Before we gather together, we are part of the natural world, we are individuals and natural families; but when we come together in one place, we become something greater than what we are as individuals. We join together with the greater spiritual family that is the Church. We leave our individual world behind us and enter into God's Kingdom.

The Liturgy therefore really begins with a separation from the world. This is something that Christians easily forget. In our attempt to make Christianity understandable and approachable to modern people, we often forget that Christ is not of this world, and therefore the Church, although in the world, is not of the world either. As the Lord said to the Apostles: "If you belonged to the world, it would love you as its own. As it is, you do not belong to the world, but I have chosen you out of the world" (John 15:19, NIV). Christianity can really only be understood from within. In other words, one must become a Christian to understand Christianity. Christ said as much to His Apostles: "To you has been given to know the mysteries of the Kingdom, but to others I speak in parables" (Lk. 8:10, VP). Admittedly, this makes it difficult to debate with nonbelievers about the value of faith, or the validity of belief in God, but we should accept this natural limitation. It is also a profound blessing! Those who come in will see why.

The Divine Liturgy, like the gospel itself, is one of the mysteries of the Faith. It is, in fact, the "Mystery of Mysteries." The Liturgy is, then, in a profound sense, not a public thing. You cannot grasp its meaning and importance from simply reading a written account of it any more than you could understand the love of a husband and wife for each other by viewing what they once wrote to each other. It expresses not human society, not our own individual personalities, concerns, and interests; rather, it reveals the heavenly Kingdom. It is, above all, the Kingdom of Heaven on earth. Therefore, it is for those who have, in a sense, already become a part of God's Kingdom through baptism. And if Christians are to bear effective witness to Christ, they must remember that they are called to point beyond this world to the Kingdom of God, to lead and guide people to that Kingdom of the Trinity.

Thus the Liturgy begins: "Blessed is the Kingdom of the Father and of the Son and of the Holy Spirit." To bless something is to rejoice in it—to receive it in love, praise, and thanksgiving—to recognize it as a means of communion with God.

The Kingdom of God is the goal of our life and of our Liturgy. The acceptance of this truth, the assent of the whole Church to the blessing and acclamation of the Kingdom made by the priest, is then proclaimed by the people with one simple word, *Amen*.

We hear this word so frequently that we are inclined to overlook its importance. But don't. The fact that this response, *Amen*, is usually made by the chanters on behalf of the people (in the vast majority of Orthodox churches there is no congregational singing) can also make us think that it is simply another extra or meaningless "churchy" word, which the choir sings simply to add a nice, big ending to the prayers and petitions. But no. *Amen* is the testimony of the whole congregation to all that is said and done by the clergy in the Liturgy. We should be fully conscious as we say it. *Amen* is usually sung by the chanters for aesthetic and practical reasons, but this word belongs to us all. Without this *Amen* of the people, literally nothing can be done in church.

The Liturgy is not a performance by the priest and chanters for the people to simply watch and listen to. *Liturgy* literally means "the work of the people." Without the laity, there is no liturgy. A priest on his own cannot celebrate a liturgy at all. There can be no Church without priests, but there can be no priests without the Church, and as I said at the beginning, the real meaning of the word *Church* is not a temple, not a church building, but the gathering of the Faithful.

The Liturgy as just this kind of joyful, Eucharistic gathering has been well expressed by two of the most important Christian theologians from the last century, Fr. Alexander Schmemann and Romano Guardini:

> The Liturgy is before all else the joyful gathering of those who are to meet the risen Lord and enter into His Kingdom. And it is this joy of expectation and this expectation of joy that are expressed in singing and ritual, in vestments and in censing, in that whole beauty of the liturgy which has so often been denounced as unnecessary and even sinful.
>
> Unnecessary it is indeed, for we are beyond the categories of the "necessary." Beauty is never "necessary," "functional" or "useful." And when, expecting someone whom we love, we put a beautiful tablecloth on the table and decorate it with candles and flowers, we do all this not out of necessity, but out of love. And the Church is love, expectation and joy. It is heaven on earth. . . . It is the joy of recovered childhood, that free, unconditioned and disinterested joy which alone is capable of transforming the world.[2]

The Liturgy, then, "speaks measuredly and melodiously; it employs formal, rhythmic gestures; it is clothed in colors and garments foreign to everyday life. . . . It is in the highest sense the life of a child, in which everything is picture, melody and song."[3]

Most of us, by contrast,

> ask for definitions and justifications, and they are rooted in fear—fear of corruption, deviation, "pagan influences," whatnot. But "he that feareth is not made perfect in love" [1 Jn. 4:18]. As long as Christians will *love* the Kingdom of God, and not only discuss it, they will "represent" it and signify it, in art and beauty. And the celebrant of the sacrament of joy will appear in a beautiful chasuble, because he is vested in the glory of the Kingdom, because even in the form of man God appears in glory. In the Eucharist we are standing in the presence of Christ, and like Moses before God, we are to be covered with his glory.[4]

⸻

········▶ The clergy at the Divine Liturgy wear vestments (garments worn specifically for this and other services). The chasuble is the outer garment worn by priests. Orthodox vestments are often elaborate, but this is not to be showy or to satisfy the priest's vanity, though that can be a temptation for clergy! There are historical and theological reasons for these special garments, as well as aesthetic ones. There is nothing run-of-the-mill or mundane about the Liturgy, nor should there be!

The Litany of Peace

So we have gathered together in order to discover our true identity; we have announced our destination: the Kingdom of the Trinity. And the people have confirmed our journey's end with the word *Amen*. Then the deacon, who usually stands between the priests and the people, between the altar and the main body of the church (divided by the iconostasis, or "icon screen"), commands us to pray in what is called the Great Litany, known also as the "Litany of Peace," because in the first three petitions we ask for peace.

> In peace let us pray to the Lord.
> For the peace from on high and for the salvation of our souls, let us pray to the Lord.
> For the peace of the whole world, for the welfare of the holy Churches of God, and for the union of all, let us pray to the Lord.

That word, *peace*, is so very important throughout our worship, throughout our lives as Christians. "Peace," writes Fr. Ephrem Lash,

> a word which is used some thirty times in the Liturgy, is not simply an absence of conflict. It is to live in harmony with God, with oneself, with all mankind and with the natural world of which we are part. It is above all a

gift from God, which, as St Paul writes to the Philippians, "is beyond all understanding." It is the gift that comes with the birth of Jesus, as the angels' hymn proclaims, "Glory to God in the highest, and peace on earth, goodwill among men." It is how Jesus sends away those he has healed or forgiven, "Go in peace." It is how he greets the Apostles after his resurrection and it is how the bishop and priest greet the people in all the services.[5]

Peace to you. Peace is necessary for prayer and worship. This is a most basic and necessary truth, and one that demonstrates how the originators of our worship, millennia ago, had a profound understanding of the human heart. If we are not at peace with God, with one another, and with ourselves, we cannot focus on prayer; and if we have hatred and animosity toward others, our prayers are not acceptable to God. This need for peace is reiterated time and again in the Divine Liturgy.

As we begin the Liturgy, then, we must put aside all our grudges; we must forgive one another; we must be at peace, that we may offer an acceptable sacrifice to God. Only then can we be made worthy to hear the Holy Gospel, to be forgiven by God, and to receive the Body and Blood of Christ in Holy Communion for the remission of sins and eternal life.

And so, even though the Church is necessarily apart from the world, in but not *of* the world, this separation is not inspired by hatred or apathy, but by the exact opposite. We leave the world that we may return to it renewed and illumined, fit to bring light to those in darkness.

❖ 2 ❖
The Great Litany

For God's grace to come during the Liturgy,
you must be concentrated and untroubled.
—Elder Amphilochios Makris

After we ask for the peace of God within us, in the world, and within the Church, we pray for "this holy house, and for those who enter it with faith, reverence and the fear of God." This is the spirit in which we come to church.

We enter the church with faith. The Divine Liturgy is above all for believers, for those who believe in God and in the teachings and ways of the Orthodox Church. We come to church for Christ, to enter into a deeper relationship with Him, and through Him our relations with one another are transformed into a relationship of divine love and communion.

We enter the church with reverence—with respect for the church building as the house of God. As St. Germanus of Constantinople once wrote:

2. *Deacon saying the Great Litany*

The Church is the temple of God, a sacred precinct, a house of prayer, the assembly of the people, the body of Christ. Its name is the bride of Christ. It has been cleansed by the water of His baptism, sprinkled by His blood and adorned in bridal array, and sealed with the ointment of the Holy Spirit. . . . The church is an earthly heaven, in which the God beyond the heavens dwells and walks about. It represents the crucifixion, burial and resurrection of Christ: it is glorified more than Moses' tabernacle of witness, in which were the mercy seat and the Holy of Holies. It is prefigured in the patriarchs, foretold in the prophets, perfected by the apostles, adorned by the hierarchs and fulfilled in martyrs.[6]

We enter the church with fear of God. When we speak of the fear of God, we should not understand this in the sense of being paralyzed with fear, of being gripped with terror at the thought of God. We know that our God is a God of love and mercy, "slow to anger, abounding in love" (Ps. 102:8 [103:8], NIV). Yet we know also that God is all-powerful and greater than us beyond imagining. Being in the presence of God is like being in the middle of the ocean, overwhelmed by the size and power of the sea, in awe of its might and magnificence. And so before God we stand in awe—with fear, wonder, and adoration.

▶ You may have noticed that one of the first things Orthodox Christians do when they enter a church is kiss the icons. Icons are a significant feature of Orthodox worship and theology. A traditional Orthodox Church is normally full of icons, frescoes, or mosaics. The icons depict Christ, His mother, and His saints. The theology of the icon is rooted in the doctrine of the Incarnation: since God became a man—flesh and blood like you and me—and was seen by human eyes, He can be depicted. The saints are those who have attained His likeness, and so the icons of the saints reveal the full implications of the Incarnation: God took on the likeness of the human being so that human beings could attain the likeness of God. Thus icons are not realistic portraits—rather, they portray human nature restored to its original beauty and proper "image." These icons "stand in" for the saints depicted. So when we enter a church, we feel that we are in the presence of the company of heaven—that they are praying and worshiping with us. We show our love and veneration for Christ and the saints through their images—by going up to them and kissing them, just as we would our dearest friends.

With these emotions and intentions we have come to church to pray and worship. Then we begin by praying for our bishop, for the honored order of presbyters (the priests), for the diaconate in Christ (the deacons), for all the clergy and the people. In every service of the Orthodox Church, we commemorate the bishop whether he is present or not. This is of great importance to the understanding of the Church. In the early Church it was the bishop, and not the priest, who would normally celebrate the Divine Liturgy. Inasmuch as the Eucharist is above all the Sacrament of the unity of the people of God, the person who leads the service would be the one whose ministry consists in preserving this unity. In the early Church, there was no parish system, with many churches in one area each holding a separate Liturgy. The Eucharist was held in one church with the bishop, and the deacons would distribute Holy Communion to those Christians in the area who were unable to be present. At the center of the Church's unity is the local bishop, because it is the bishop who presides at the Eucharist, which is the heart of the Church's life.

The priests and deacons are merely the assistants and delegates of the bishop. Their ministry is not their own but is the ministry of the bishop, which they carry out on his behalf. St. Ignatius, in the early second century, wrote: "Let no one do anything involving the church without the bishop. . . . Let the congregation be wherever the bishop is; just as wherever Jesus Christ is, there is the universal church." But St. Ignatius also writes, "Let that eucharist be considered valid that occurs under the bishop or the one to whom he entrusts it."[7]

Already by the beginning of the second century there were times when a bishop could not celebrate the

Liturgy and delegated the task to one of his priests. In time, the exception became the rule. "The bishop was gradually transformed from the leader of a concrete church community into an administrator of a more or less extensive ecclesiastical area"[8] (a diocese), and so began the administrative organization of a number of churches under the rule of one bishop.

In the conscience of most Christians today, it is the priest and not the bishop that has come to be seen as the "pastor," the "shepherd" of the flock, while the bishop is perceived as the "superior" of the clergy, a distant administrator of the Church, rather than its chief priest and spiritual father. "Thus it is characteristic that we call the priest, not the bishop, 'father,' while we greet the bishop as 'master.'"[9] And yet, even though the priest has replaced the bishop as the normal celebrant of the Eucharist, the Orthodox Church has never forgotten that it is the bishop, and not the priest, who is the center of church unity.

In that spirit, before the opening blessing of the Liturgy, even when the bishop is absent, the deacon proclaims, "Master, give the blessing." The preservation of this command to the bishop to begin the Liturgy reminds us that the priest who celebrates the Liturgy does so on behalf of the bishop. It is through the bishop that all of our local churches, all of our parishes, are united. "The calling and essence of the episcopate," says Schmemann, "consists in ensuring that no one community, no single 'parish' becomes self-contained, shut up in itself,"[10] cut off from the life of the rest of the Church. It is through the bishop that all of our churches and parishes, their clergy and congregations, are linked together and united as one single Church. This is the meaning of commemorating the bishop at the Divine Liturgy.

We then continue by commemorating the local authorities, heeding the words of St. Paul: "I exhort that prayers be made for all people, for rulers and for all that are in authority, that we may lead a quiet and peaceable life in all godliness and honesty" (1 Tim. 2:1–2, VP).

We pray for the area in which we live, "for every city, town, and village, and for the faithful who dwell in them."

We pray "for favourable weather, an abundance of the fruits of the earth, and temperate seasons."

We pray for travelers, the sick, the suffering, the imprisoned, and for their salvation.

It is worth noting that the word *salvation* in Greek (*soteria*) has a double meaning. Its first and original meaning is "safety" or "protection." In some of our hymns and prayers to the Mother of God, we ask her to "save" us. This is not because we believe that she is the one who grants salvation to humanity in the theological sense of the word. We ask for her protection, through her prayers and loving care for humanity and the world. But salvation also came to be understood in the theological sense that humanity is redeemed, saved from sin and reunited with God. In this sense, Christ is our only salvation.

Finally, we ask for "our deliverance from all affliction, wrath, danger, and constraint."

After each petition, the choir sings, "Lord, have mercy" (in Greek, *Kyrie eleison*).

In the previous chapter I explained that the word *Amen*, though usually sung by the choir, belongs to all of us. It is the response of the people to all that is said and done by the clergy. This is true also of the words *Lord, have mercy*.

Although it is undoubtedly beautiful, the Great Litany is not a musical performance by the clergy and choir. The deacon leading us in prayer intones, "In peace, let us pray to the Lord," and with each command to pray, we respond with the words *Lord, have mercy*. Some Orthodox Christians respond also in the physical action of making the sign of the cross. In this sense, we all participate. We are not at the Liturgy as if it were a concert, simply to listen, but to act, to pray. Such is the importance of the responses of the chanters and of our acts of prayer such as crossing ourselves, lighting candles, and making prostrations or small bows during the services.

The Great Litany ends: "Commemorating our all-holy, pure, most blessed, and glorious Lady Mother of God and ever-virgin Mary, with all the saints, let us entrust ourselves and one another and our lives to Christ our God."

In the Great Litany, as in all prayers of the Church, we pray as one for that which is necessary for us all (peace, favorable weather, the fruits of the earth), for those in need (the sick, the suffering, the imprisoned), and for our safety and salvation. We respond to these petitions by asking only for God's mercy and nothing more, heeding the words of our Lord: "When you pray, do not use meaningless repetition . . . for your Father knows what you need before you ask Him" (Matt. 6:7–8, VP). And "Do not worry, saying, 'What shall we eat?' or 'What shall we drink?' or 'What shall we wear?' . . . Your heavenly Father knows that you need these things. But seek first his kingdom and his righteousness, and all these things shall be yours as well. Therefore do not worry about tomorrow, for tomorrow will worry about itself. Let the day's own trouble be sufficient for the day" (Matt. 6:31–33, VP).

Thus, with faith, reverence, and fear of God, we entrust ourselves and one another, and our whole life, to Christ our God.

3. *Priest leading the Divine Liturgy*

❖ 3 ❖
The Mini Creed

Praise the Lord, o my soul: while I live
I will praise the Lord; while I exist I
will praise my God.
—Ps. 145:1–2 [146:1–2], EL

O ur surroundings may be magnificent: icons all around us and looking down upon us, the voices of the clergy and choir soaring; or we may be in a church that is not so magnificent, with clergy and chanters who are not so musically talented. But however splendid the service may be, our prayer is simple. Some may be praying in attentive silence, others in movement—by making the sign of the cross—while yet others may be remembering specific people or needs during the Litany. Either way, we are praying together. And once the Great Litany ends, we are all drawn into a common act of worship and veneration, in a part of the service called the antiphons (a Greek word meaning "opposite voices"). These antiphons are refrains with psalm verses sung in alternation by the chanters and interspersed with what is called the Little Litany.

Again and again in peace let us pray to the Lord.

Help us, save us, have mercy on us, and keep us O God, by your grace.

Commemorating our all-holy, most blessed and glorious lady, Mother of God and ever-virgin Mary, with all the saints, let us entrust ourselves and one another and our whole life to Christ our God.

....

After the second set of antiphons, shortly before the Entrance of the Gospel, when the clergy bring out the Gospel book in procession to the middle of the church (see chapter 4), we sing a hymn that could be called a mini Creed:

Only-begotten Son and Word of God, who, being immortal, accepted for our salvation to take flesh from the holy Mother of God and Ever-Virgin Mary, and without change became man; you were crucified, Christ God, by death trampling on death, being one of the Holy Trinity, glorified with the Father and the Holy Spirit: save us!

▶ There are three sets of antiphons, though the third is not always chanted as a refrain with the psalm verses. On most Sundays throughout the year, the refrain for the first set of antiphons is: "At the prayers of the Mother of God, Saviour, save us"; while for the second set of antiphons, the refrain is: "Son of God, risen from the dead, save us who sing to you: Alleluia!" The refrain for the third set of antiphons is the principal hymn of the day, which is chanted during the Entrance of the Gospel.

This hymn was originally the beginning of the Liturgy, an Entrance Hymn (*Eisodikon*). The phrases of this short hymn sum up some of the most basic and fundamental aspects of our Orthodox Faith. Let us pause to consider them one by one.

Only-Begotten Son and Word of God

It is important to explain this term *Word of God.* When we speak of the Word (with a capital *w*), we are not usually speaking of the gospel, or the Bible; we are not talking about the written or spoken word. Instead, we are referring to a person, to the Second Person of the Trinity. We read at the beginning of St. John's Gospel:

In the beginning was the Word, and the Word was with God, and the Word was God. He was with God in the beginning. Through him all things were made; without him nothing was made that has been made. In him was life, and that life was the light of all mankind. . . . He was in the world, and though the world was made through him, the world did not recognize him. He came to that which was his own, but his own did not receive him. . . . The Word became flesh and made his dwelling among us. (John 1:1–4, 10–11, 14, NIV)

St. John is referring to Jesus Christ. *The Word* is usually the term that is used for Christ before His Incarnation—that is, before His human birth. Christ is coeternal with God the Father. He always existed. He is, as we say in the Creed, "begotten of the Father before all ages. Light from Light, true God from true God."

Christ is not a mere prophet or moral teacher. He is God Himself, one of the Trinity. We have one God, and yet our God is not one person, but three persons in one Godhead.

When we use the terms *Father* and *Son* in the Trinity, we must not get confused with how we normally think of father-son relationships. It does not mean that once there was just the Father, and then the Son came along. These terms, *Father* and *Son*, help us to understand the eternal relationship between the persons of the Trinity, but they cannot be pushed too far or be taken too literally.

The Son and the Holy Spirit are coeternal with the Father. God was always, is always, and will always be Trinity. But it is the second person of the Trinity, the Only-begotten Son and Word of God, Who became a man and lived among us. It is because of this act of God becoming a human being like us that we are able to become one with God.

Who, Being Immortal, Accepted for Our Salvation to Take Flesh from the Holy Mother of God and Ever-Virgin Mary

The veneration of the Virgin Mary as Mother of God (*Theotokos*) is firmly rooted in the doctrine of the Incarnation—that is, the human birth of the eternal Son of God, Jesus Christ. In the very word *Theotokos* is revealed the mystery of the Incarnation. The Virgin Mary gave birth to God in the flesh, one person with two natures—human and divine. Since the salvation of the world through the Incarnation was effected by God through the Virgin Mary, we venerate her as the Mother of our God and as the ultimate example of synergy—of cooperation with God's will. She is humankind's offering to God, from whom He took flesh for our salvation.

We venerate the Mother of God always in light of her role in the Incarnation. We do not venerate her simply on account of her own virtue but in virtue of the fact that Christ entered the world through her. This is why most icons of the Mother of God show her with Christ in her arms.

Some non-Orthodox Christians are not comfortable with the veneration of the Mother of God. Many wonder, does all of this veneration of the Virgin Mary somehow overshadow Jesus Christ? I have found this to be an almost knee-jerk reaction of some people when looking upon the significant position of the Virgin Mary in Orthodox worship.

The simple fact of the matter is this: there would be no Jesus without Mary. To venerate the Virgin Mary is to revere Christ becoming a man for our salvation, to fall down in awe before the great mystery of the Incarnation. He Whom heaven itself, even the highest heaven, could not contain is contained in the womb of a young woman! The Ancient of Days becomes a newborn child. He Who existed before the world began is born of a virgin. How can we worship God without revering His coming to earth and revealing Himself to us as flesh and blood? But how can we remember this without remembering the woman from whom He took flesh? And how can we remember her without wonder and adoration? This is why we have such a profound reverence for the Mother of God. For in this very word *Theotokos* is contained the whole mystery of the Incarnation and the salvation of the human race.

The Mother of God is hailed also as Ever-Virgin (*Aeiparthenos*). The Church Fathers and hymns refer repeatedly to this paradox: virginity and motherhood are in nature mutually exclusive, but in the Mother of God the two opposites meet and are joined together. Christ was born not of man but of the Holy Spirit, and Orthodox Tradition, like Catholicism, holds that the Mother of God remained a virgin after the Birth of Christ as well as before. Some Christians contest this, quoting as their argument a passage in the Gospel of Matthew (13:54–56): "When [Jesus] had come to His own country, He taught them in their synagogue, so that they were astonished and said, 'Where did this Man get this wisdom and these mighty works? Is this not the carpenter's son? Is not His mother called Mary? And His brothers James, Joses, Simon, and Judas? And His sisters, are they not all with us? Where then did this man get all these things?'" (NKJV).

Orthodoxy understands these brothers and sisters as "siblings" from a former wife of Joseph, and not from Mary. Furthermore, "The terminology of Israel . . . made no distinction between brothers and cousins but referred to all as 'brothers.'"[11] Mary had become the mother of all humankind through giving birth to God. She belonged completely and utterly to Him:

Becoming the vessel for the Lord of Glory Himself, and carrying in the flesh Him whom heaven and earth cannot contain, surely would have been grounds to consider her life, including her body, as fully consecrated to God and sexual relations as unthinkable. Even in the comparatively minor (and strikingly parallel) incident of the Lord's entry through the East gate of the Temple in Ezekiel 43–44, prompts the call: "This gate shall be shut; it shall not be opened, and no one shall enter by it, for the Lord God of Israel has entered by it; therefore it shall be shut" (44:2).[12]

And Without Change Became Man

The Word of God, in becoming man, did not cease to be God. In Christ God and man, divinity and humanity, are joined. Christ is like the bridge between God and man, between heaven and earth. For only if He is God can we come to the Father through Him, but only if He is human can we humans meet with God through Him.

You Were Crucified, Christ God, by Death Trampling on Death

Humanity, through its own sin, through disobedience to God's will, had become mortal, subject to death. So Christ, Who is immortal, became a mortal and died, that He may destroy death, because He is greater than death. He is the source of life. He is life itself. Thus by His own death, which could only be achieved by becoming a mortal man, He destroyed death, and He granted us immortality once more; as God death has no power over Him. He rose from the dead and ascended to the Father in heaven, that we too, after our death, may ascend there to be with Him. As it is written in the Gospel of St. John: "In my Father's house are many rooms. . . . I am going there to prepare a place for you. And if I go and prepare a place for you, I will come back and take you to be with me that you also may be where I am" (14:2–3, vp). One of the greatest teachers and bishops of the Church, St. Athanasius the Great, summed this all up very well by saying: "God became man that man might become God."[13]

All this is the source of our joy and hope, the heart of our faith. Through Christ, we are given true, everlasting life. Therefore at the Divine Liturgy, we give thanks, we praise and worship the author of our salvation. We offer our lives to Him, that we may have true life, that Christ may always be with us and within us. That is the ultimate purpose of the Eucharist. At the Liturgy, Christ is incarnated again, no longer in the form of a man, but now in the form of bread and wine, that in Holy Communion we may be able to receive Him as His Body and Blood and thus be perfectly and fully one with Him.

Of course, at the beginning of the Liturgy we are far from reaching the point of Holy Communion. But the Liturgy is our preparation for Communion.

We must not separate the Sacrament of the Eucharist from the Liturgy. For there can be no Holy Communion without the Liturgy. Of course, Communion is taken to those who are sick, who are physically unable to come to church to partake in the Divine Liturgy. But otherwise we must participate in the Liturgy before we can receive Communion.

But before we even begin to speak of Holy Communion at the Divine Liturgy, we must first hear the word of God, and this hearing of God's word is also something that we must prepare for, and that preparation begins with what is called the "Little Entrance," or the "Entrance of the Gospel," when the clergy bring the Gospel from the altar and carry it in procession to the center of the church.

4

Entrance of the Gospel

You give wisdom and understanding
to those who ask.
—Prayer of the Trisagion,
Liturgy of St. John Chrysostom

The procession to the center of the church that we call the "Entrance of the Gospel" is a profound moment at the service of the Divine Liturgy. This is the moment when the clergy take the Gospel book from the altar and bring it out among the people.

The central focus and high point of the first half of the Liturgy is the Gospel Reading. This is so thoroughly important to us because the Orthodox Church is a scriptural church. It is founded upon the Gospel of Christ. Alas, many Orthodox Christians are apt to forget this. Some get so caught up in the rites and rituals, in the splendor and worship, that they sometimes forget that the Orthodox Church is, in the truest sense of the word, "evangelical," that is, it is rooted in the Gospel, the Good News that God became

4. *Entrance of the Gospel*

a man, destroyed death by death, and rose from the dead, granting Resurrection to all humanity.

The Entrance of the Gospel was once the starting point of the Liturgy. It was the Entrance not only of the Gospel but also of the people. In the early days of the Church, all of the people on Sundays and great feast days would gather together in one church rather than in their segregated parish churches. The people proceeded from their own parish churches or homes to the cathedral church or the church that was celebrating its feast day, singing hymns as they went. In those days, when Christians were still subject to persecution by the Romans, the Gospel book was not kept in the church as it is today, since there was a danger of its being confiscated and destroyed. Instead it was brought to the church from outside. Once the Gospel had been carried to the bishop who was to celebrate the Liturgy, the bishop would bless the people and the Liturgy would begin. The Entrance of the Gospel in the Liturgy today, when the clergy carry the Gospel from the altar in a small procession to the middle of the church, is the last remnant of this ancient practice.

There are two Scripture readings in most Orthodox liturgies—one from the Epistles and one from the Gospels. In the past there were more than two, including readings from the Old Testament. But the high point of the first half of the Liturgy has always been the Gospel Reading.

> ▶ The Gospel book is kept on the Holy Altar. It contains the readings from the four Gospels for every day of the year. It is usually bound in metal with an icon or engraving of the Crucifixion on the one side and of the Resurrection on the other.

The Thrice-Holy Hymn

But before we hear the readings from the Scriptures, the Church invites us to enter into God's presence. The Church has always known that it is very difficult for people to shift from their normal state of mind, one that is made up of anxiety and stress, of busy schedules and mindless recreation, into a more spiritual, calmer state of mind; and it is such a state of mind that we need to have if we are to be open to hearing and understanding God's word in the biblical readings in church. Therefore, shortly after the Entrance of the Gospel, once we have chanted the main hymns of the day, we chant one of the most ancient hymns of the Church, a hymn known as the Trisagion, or "thrice-holy" hymn:

Holy God, Holy Strong, Holy Immortal, have mercy on us.

This hymn brings to mind a hymn of the angels in heaven that was heard by the prophet Isaiah:

> I saw the Lord, high and exalted, seated on a throne; and the train of his robe filled the temple. Above him were seraphim, each with six wings: With two wings they covered their faces, with two they covered their feet, and with two they were flying. And they were calling to one another: "Holy, holy, holy is the LORD Almighty; the whole earth is full of his glory." (Isa. 6:1–4, NIV)

The thrice-holy hymn of the angels was also heard by the Apostle John, as recorded in the Book of Revelation: "Day and night they never stop saying: 'Holy, holy, holy is the Lord God Almighty, who was, and is, and is to come'" (Rev. 4:8, NIV).

With this hymn the Church takes us up into the Kingdom of God. We are surrounded, as it were, by the angelic host. What a powerful moment this is! Our Liturgy on earth is joined with the eternal liturgy in heaven. This is why, at the Entrance of the Gospel, the priest prays:

> Master, Lord our God, you have set orders and armies of Angels and Archangels in heaven to minister to your glory; grant that, with our entrance, holy Angels may enter, concelebrating with us, and with us glorifying your goodness.

"The angels are not here for decoration and inspiration," writes Fr. Alexander Schmemann:

> They stand precisely for heaven, for that glorious and incomprehensible above and beyond of which we know only one thing: that it eternally resounds with the praise of divine glory and holiness: 'Holy' is the real name of God, of the God 'not of scholars and philosophers' but of the living God of faith. The knowledge *about* God results in definitions and distinctions. The knowledge *of* God leads to this one, incomprehensible, yet obvious and inescapable word: holy. And in this word we express both that God is the Absolutely Other, the One about whom we know nothing, and that He is the end of all our hunger, all our desires, the inaccessible One who mobilizes our wills, the mysterious treasure that attracts us, and there is really nothing to know but Him. "Holy" is the word, the song, the "reaction" of the Church as it enters into heaven, as it stands before the heavenly glory of God.[14]

The Readings

After the Trisagion, the deacon commands, "Let us attend!" and the Reader acclaims the Epistle reading for the day. "Let us attend." We often hear this command at particularly important and solemn moments in our services, and it is said before every reading. The purpose of this simple phrase is clear: It is God's word we are listening to. We should pay special attention! Sometimes in contrast, you will hear people chatting during the Epistle reading in some Greek Orthodox churches; this is nothing new. Even in the fourth century, St. John Chrysostom was complaining about it: "There stands the deacon crying aloud and saying, 'Let us attend!' and yet no one pays attention!"[15]

Traditionally, the Epistle and Gospel Readings are not merely read but intoned, chanted. The first reason for this is, as I said, because it is God's word we are hearing. We are not listening to an article from a newspaper or magazine, but to a sacred text, and so it is read in a way that is unusual, not in the same way we read and hear other texts. The second reason is to be audible. Bear in mind that for centuries there were no microphones in church, and in great cathedrals and basilicas, it was necessary that the readings be intoned in order for all to hear clearly. A third reason, according to Fr. Ephrem Lash, "is because the Reader is simply a transmitter, it is not up to him to put his own slant on the text, to put himself, as it were, between God and the listener. It is God's word that we have come to hear, and not the reader's, be he Bishop, Priest, Deacon or Layman. They are simply loud speakers, not the authors."[16]

The Epistle is then followed by the "Alleluaria"— the chanting of Alleluias with psalm verses, though in many churches the full chanting of the Alleluaria has been replaced by three quick, simple Alleluias.

The Alleluaria is a preparation for the reading of the Gospel. As the choir sings, the deacon censes the altar, the icons, and the people, and then he makes his way with the book of Gospels to the pulpit to proclaim the Gospel from there. This preparation for hearing the Gospel, the importance of the Gospel Reading, and, indeed, the whole purpose of the Liturgy until this point is summed up in a prayer that the priest says during the Alleluaria:

> Master, Lover of mankind, make the pure light of your divine knowledge shine in our hearts and open the eyes of our mind to understand the message of your Gospel. Implant in us the fear of your blessed commandments, so that, having trampled down all carnal desires, we may pursue a spiritual way of life, thinking and doing all things that are pleasing to you. For you are the illumination of our souls and

bodies, Christ God, and to you we give glory, together with your Father who is without beginning, and your all-holy, good and life-giving Spirit, now and for ever, and to the ages of ages. Amen.

The hearing of the Gospel is not something that the Orthodox take lightly. In our services, there is always a sense of needing to be prepared and made worthy to hear and comprehend it. Even at the service of Matins, when the Gospel is read, it is introduced with the words, "And that we may be accounted worthy to hear the holy Gospel, let us entreat the Lord our God." So too at the Liturgy, we pray and prepare that we may hear God's word, understand it, and take it to heart. Then the Gospel for the day is chanted aloud.

5. *Deacon chanting the Gospel*

✦ 5 ✦
Catechumens

And I have other sheep that are not of this fold.
I must bring them also, and they will listen to my
voice. So there will be one flock, one shepherd.
—JOHN 10:16, ESV

The first half of the Liturgy is known as the Liturgy of the Word, because its central focus is the Gospel, but it is also known as the Liturgy of the Catechumens. It is important to understand what this means if we are to understand the part of the service that follows the Gospel Reading.

This word, *catechumen,* is one that has almost entirely disappeared from English vocabulary. It has almost entirely fallen into disuse in the Church's vocabulary as well. What are, or what were, catechumens?

A catechumen was someone who was being instructed in the Faith and being prepared to become a member of the Church, someone who was being "catechized," that is, instructed, in order eventually to be baptized. Catechumens were a particular order of

Christians—Christians who believed and who wished to become full-fledged, baptized Christians but who were not yet ready for this. Their instruction in the Christian Faith from the time they were made catechumens until their baptism would usually last for one to three years, though instruction continued after baptism also.

During those one or more years, the teachings, doctrines, practices, and Scriptures of the Church would be taught and explained to them. Part of that instruction was the first part of the Liturgy. The Readings from the Scriptures were therefore a form of "Bible study" for the catechumens, and this Bible study included a sermon after the readings had been heard. The original and correct place of the sermon was therefore immediately after the Gospel Reading. The first reason for this is that the sermon has always been understood as an extension of the Gospel message, or as an explanation of the Readings. The second reason is that the catechumens, as I will explain a little later, were dismissed from the church shortly after the sermon. They were not permitted to participate in the Liturgy from this point on. The sermon, therefore, was originally an instruction in the Faith mainly intended for the catechumens.

In many churches it is common for the sermon to be given much later, before the Communion of the people or just before the end of the Liturgy. The only reason for this is unfortunately that many of the Faithful

▶ In the Liturgy of the Presanctified Gifts, from the middle of Lent, we have prayers for a specific group of catechumens—"those being prepared for enlightenment" (*oi pros to photisma*). Catechumens were normally baptized at the Paschal (Easter) Liturgy. Mid-Lent was the time of the "great scrutiny," when it was decided whether a catechumen was ready to be baptized. The *pros to photisma* were those catechumens who were prepared for baptism.

▶ It is not very common for Orthodox Christians to all turn up at the Liturgy at the same time. There is no sense of having to be there from the very beginning of the service. While latecomers no doubt miss out, and while this can sometimes be a source of noise and distraction for those who are already engaged in the Liturgy, it also testifies to the fact that Orthodox Christians enjoy a certain freedom in church. After all, we are children in our Father's house.

are not in church early enough for the Gospel. But the Epistle and Gospel Readings were for the benefit not only of the catechumens but for everyone. It is a sad reality that many Orthodox Christians today are not anywhere near as familiar with the Scriptures as they should be. Not only do many not read or have never read the Bible at home, but many also do not come to church early enough to hear the New Testament Readings at the Liturgy.

After the Gospel Reading, we begin a part of the Liturgy that in most Greek Orthodox churches is omitted or not audible to the people. The part of the Liturgy I am referring to is the prayers for and dismissal of the catechumens. The deacon says: "Catechumens, pray to the Lord. . . . Believers, let us pray for the catechumens," and eventually we hear the deacon proclaim, "Catechumens, depart! . . . None of the catechumens!"

Why were the catechumens told to leave the church? Why could they not take part in the Liturgy beyond this point? The reason is that the second half of the Liturgy, called the Liturgy of the Faithful, or the Liturgy of the Holy Gifts, is all about Holy Communion—it is the preparation for Communion—and it is impossible to receive Communion before baptism. Therefore the catechumens, who were not yet baptized, were ordered to leave the church.

I am not explaining all of this simply as a history lesson but in order to draw attention to two things quite fundamental about the Church and the Liturgy that many Orthodox Christians have largely forgotten.

The first thing we have forgotten is the role that instruction and learning should play—and once played—in the fulfillment of the Church's mission and purpose in this world: to carry out the commandment of our Lord, "Go therefore and make disciples of all nations, baptizing them in the name of the Father, and of the Son, and of the Holy Spirit, teaching them to observe all that I have commanded you" (Matt. 28:19–20, ESV). The reason that in most churches the prayers for and dismissal of the catechumens are omitted is that the order of catechumens no longer exists. Surely this should be a cause for concern. How is it that the instruction of catechumens—which for so many centuries was such an important aspect of Church life that the Liturgy itself was, to an extent, structured around them and designed to teach them and integrate them into the Church—has simply disappeared from the Church's life?

In the early Church, infant baptism was rare. Adult baptism was the norm, and baptism was impossible without prior instruction. But even those who were baptized in infancy were instructed in the Faith as they grew up. There is evidence for infant baptism from the earliest times: in the Acts of the Apostles, for example, we read that households (which surely included children) were baptized (Acts 18:8); St. Justin Martyr, in the middle of the second century, wrote: "Both men and women who have been Christ's disciples since childhood, remain pure."[17] St. John Chrysostom, in the fourth century, not long after Christianity was made legal, refers to the practice of baptizing children: "We do baptise children, although they are not guilty of any sins."[18] But gradually, instead of infant and adult baptism existing side-by-side, infant baptism came to almost entirely replace adult baptism. So for centuries there was, perhaps, little room for catechumens in Orthodox countries, where just about everyone was baptized in infancy. But in our twenty-first-century context in the West—living as we do in what are non-Orthodox countries, and countries that are rapidly losing any kind of Christian identity, in which more and more people are being taught virtually nothing of Christianity or, perhaps worse still, have been taught wrongly—the absence of catechumens is a real cause for concern.

Converts and Baptism

It is common for people to convert to the Orthodox Church, but all too often such people are received without instruction and, far worse than this, without a sincere belief in the Orthodox Church. Many are baptized with very little if any instruction simply in order to marry an Orthodox partner. I said earlier that catechumens were instructed for one to three years before baptism. Well, it was not easy to get baptized. One's faith was scrutinized, and one could not become a member of the Church without learning, conviction, and dedication. It is probably time that we once again began to take baptism more seriously.

As a kind of corollary, it is also high time—today, in our twenty-first-century Western contexts—that we began looking beyond our little world of ethnic groups and families (Greeks, Russians, Serbs, Arabs, and the rest) and once again began thinking in terms of "making disciples of all nations." The media likes to give the impression that the days of religion are numbered, that people are simply not interested in religion or spirituality anymore. But this is not true. There is a great thirst for religion and spirituality all around us. People are turning more and more to religion or spirituality in some form or another. And where are the Orthodox in the midst of all this desperate searching? We too often seem to hide behind closed doors, celebrating our own private customs and rituals, hidden from the world, unwilling or ashamed to open our doors to the outside world, to make our Orthodox Faith and Tradition heard and known.

The Importance of Communion

The second fundamental thing that the catechumens, and specifically the dismissal of the catechumens, reminds us of is that the whole purpose of the second half of the Liturgy is Holy Communion.

It once was that only those who were able to receive Communion could participate in the Liturgy of the Holy Gifts. Furthermore, those baptized Christians who were excommunicated—who had committed very grievous sins that prohibited them from receiving

Communion—also left the main part of the church. In other words, anyone who was in church from this point onward was there to receive Communion, and anyone who was not to receive Communion had no business being there.

This is not to say that those who do not receive Communion should leave the church—it is not that we should necessarily return to this ancient practice—but it is worth mentioning because it illustrates that the idea of simply attending the Liturgy without receiving Communion, though it has become common practice, should not be the norm. What we must do to receive Communion I will explain in detail in chapter 8. For now, I simply want to stress that we must not separate Communion from the Liturgy. We come to the Liturgy above all to receive Communion.

In the following chapter we will look at the second part of the Liturgy—the Liturgy of the Faithful—in which we prepare for Holy Communion.

⬢

⋯⋯⋯▶ As the Liturgy of the Catechumens draws to an end, the Gospel book is put to one side, and a square cloth, called the eiliton, or the antimension, is opened upon the altar. This is the cloth on which the Holy Gifts—the bread and wine of the Eucharist—are placed. The antimension is signed by the local bishop, with the blessing of whom the Liturgy is celebrated.

❦ 6 ❦

The Cherubic Hymn and Entrance of the Holy Gifts

*Where Christ is, there are the angels too, and where
Christ and the angels are, there is Heaven.*
—St. John Chrysostom

Until now, we have been experiencing the first part of the Liturgy—the Liturgy of the Word. After the Gospel Reading and dismissal of the catechumens, we begin the second part of the service—the Liturgy of the Holy Gifts—and for the first time since the Liturgy began, we refer to Holy Communion, in the following prayer of the clergy:

> Again and many times we fall down before you and beseech you, who are good and the lover of mankind, that heeding our prayer you will cleanse our souls and bodies from every

defilement of flesh and spirit, and will grant us to stand without guilt or condemnation before your holy altar. Give also to those who pray with us the grace of progress in right living, faith and spiritual understanding. Grant that always worshipping you with fear and love, they may partake of your holy Mysteries [that is, Holy Communion] without guilt or condemnation, and be counted worthy of your heavenly kingdom.

Orthodox Christians believe that the bread and wine of the Eucharist become the actual Body and Blood of Christ. Therefore we approach Communion with profound reverence, *with fear and love.*

The above prayer is followed by what is called the Cherubic Hymn:

We who in a mystery represent the Cherubim and sing the thrice-holy hymn to the life-giving Trinity, let us now lay aside every care of this life. For we are about to receive the King of all, invisibly escorted by the angelic hosts. Alleluia.

With this hymn, the Liturgy, if you like, changes gear. The atmosphere of the Liturgy changes—it slows down and becomes more solemn, because it is from this point that we begin to prepare for Communion, and the Sacrament of the Eucharist begins.

In order to appreciate the meaning of this beautiful hymn, we must understand what the Cherubim are. According to Christian Orthodox Tradition, the Cherubim are one of the nine orders of angels. They are the second highest of them all:

Seraphim
Cherubim
Thrones
Dominions
Virtues
Powers
Principalities
Archangels
Angels

The Cherubim and Seraphim are those angels who are closest to God. *Cherubim* means "the seat of the glory of God." In many Church texts, the Cherubim are described as the seat, or throne, of God. We find this idea in the Scriptures, in the writings of the Church Fathers, and in the Divine Liturgy itself. At one point in the Liturgy, when the bishop goes to sit on the throne behind the altar (the *ano kathedra*), he blesses it and says, "Blessed are you on the throne of glory of your Kingdom, who are seated upon the Cherubim."

The Cherubim could also be described as those angels who "carry" God, in a similar way that kings were carried upon the shoulders of their closest and most devoted servants. "They are called this," Chrysostom remarks, "not because God has need of a throne, but so that you may learn how great is the dignity of these very powers."[19]

"We who in a mystery represent the Cherubim . . ." we chant in the Cherubic Hymn. And while we chant, we watch as the clergy cense the altar, the sanctuary, and the people, and then take the paten and the chalice, which hold the bread and wine we are to offer in the Eucharist, from the sanctuary and carry them around the church in a solemn procession, called the Great Entrance.

At this point the Holy Gifts have not yet been consecrated. They are not yet the Body and Blood of Christ. But even now they already symbolize what they will become—the flesh and blood of our God. Thus it is as if the clergy are representing the Cherubim, bearing God aloft, carrying Him.

▶ The paten and chalice are the two most sacred vessels in the Church, since they hold the Body and Blood of Christ. The paten (*Diskos*) is a disc-shaped metal plate on which the bread of the Eucharist is placed.

➤ Where have the bread and wine that are carried in procession come from? Before the Liturgy begins, the clergy prepare the bread and wine in a rite called the *Proskomidi*, which takes place inside the sanctuary at a table called the *prothesis*. In this service, the bread that will become the Body of Christ is cut from the *prosforo*—a loaf of bread offered by the Faithful for the purpose of the Liturgy. The *Proskomidi* is full of scriptural symbolism. From the *prosforo* the priest cuts out the *lamb* (the portion of bread that is to be consecrated at the Eucharist—it is impressed with a seal with the first and last Greek initials of the name Jesus Christ [ICXC] and the word NIKA [conquers]) and places it on the paten while quoting the following biblical passage: "Like a sheep he was led to the slaughter and as an unblemished lamb before its shearer is dumb, so he does not open his mouth. In his humiliation judgement was denied him. For his life is taken from the earth" (Isa. 53:7–8, EL). Then, using a special knife called the *loghi*—resembling a lance—he pierces the *lamb* and quotes another biblical passage: "One of the soldiers pierced his side with a lance . . . ," pours wine and water into the chalice, and continues, ". . . and at once there came out blood and water" (John 19:34, EL). The paten and chalice are covered with veils and left on the *prothesis* until the Great Entrance.

6. *Bishop receiving the Holy Gifts at the Great Entrance*

This is yet another way that the Liturgy is a journey to the Kingdom of God. We were taken even higher into heaven with the thrice-holy hymn of the angels after the Entrance of the Gospel. Now we are taken yet even higher in the Entrance of the Holy Gifts.

Our Worship Is Truly Heavenly

Our imitation of heavenly worship in the Divine Liturgy is found not only in song and in the Great Entrance but also in the censing. As it says in St. John's Revelation: "And another angel came and stood at the altar with a golden censer. He was given much incense to offer, with the prayers of all the saints on the golden altar that is before the throne. And the smoke of the incense, with the prayers of the saints, rose before God from the hand of the angel" (8:3–4, ESV).

The censing at the altar before the throne, the chanting of the thrice-holy hymn, the carrying of the Holy Gifts—all of this is an imitation of the angelic life. The Cherubic Hymn then goes on: "Let us now lay aside every care of this life, for we are about to receive the King of all, invisibly escorted by the angelic hosts. Alleluia."

We are to begin preparing to receive the King of all, that is, to receive Christ in Holy Communion, by first of all laying aside the cares of this life. We are invited to put aside all our concerns and preoccupations and devote ourselves completely to the adoration of God.

This reminds me of the Gospel passage in which Christ is preaching and a woman called Mary is listening to his words, while her sister Martha is busy in the kitchen. Martha complains to Jesus that Mary has left her to work alone and asks Jesus to tell Mary to help her. Jesus replies, "Martha, Martha, you are worrying and fretting about many things. Only one thing is needed. Mary has chosen the better part which shall not be taken from her" (Lk. 10:41–42, EL). "At this moment of the Liturgy," writes Fr. Ephrem Lash, "we are to be Mary, who sat at Jesus' feet and listened to his words, rather than Martha."[20] We must learn to let go of all the daily preoccupations and concerns that fill our minds and take up so much of our time, that state of anxiety which has almost become second nature. We are reminded that God is the one thing that is needed. And so the Church calls us to "lay aside every care of this life that we may receive the King of all."

The Great Entrance

This brings us to one of those most beautiful moments in the service—a moment that shows how worship can express our deepest spiritual yearnings.

Halfway through the Cherubic Hymn, the choir stops, and the clergy come out with the Holy Gifts. As they carry them around the church and to the altar, they sing. "May the Lord God remember you all in His

Kingdom, always, now and forever and to the ages of ages." This brings to mind the words of the penitent thief who was crucified with Jesus: "Remember me when you come into your kingdom." To which our Lord replied, "Today you will be with me in paradise" (Lk. 23:42–43, NIV). It is repentance that opens the gates of heaven to us, as one of the most famous hymns of the *Triodion* (the main hymnbook of Lent) reminds us:

> Open to me the gates of repentance, O Giver of life. For early in the morning my spirit seeks your holy temple, bearing a temple of the body all defiled. But in your compassion cleanse it now by your loving kindness and mercy.

What is happening? We are being prepared for Communion.

There are some prayers many Orthodox Christians like to read before Communion that are reminiscent of this idea of opening the gates of repentance in order to receive Christ in the Sacrament of Communion:

> "Lord my God, I know that I am not worthy nor deserve that you should come under the roof of the house of my soul," but "as you did not disdain to go in to eat with sinners in the house of Simon the leper, so consent to enter the house of my poor soul, . . . sinner though I am."

"You give the command; I will open the gates which you alone created, and you enter with love for mankind, as is your nature; you enter and enlighten my darkened reasoning."

When the clergy place the Holy Gifts on the altar, the choir completes the Cherubic Hymn, the gifts are covered with a veil, and the priest censes them. For we are now to offer the gifts of bread and wine that they may become the Body and Blood of Christ.

❖ 7 ❖

Psalm 50

God's kindness leads you to repentance.
—Rom. 2:4, vp

The only psalm that is prescribed to be recited in its entirety at every Divine Liturgy is Psalm 50 (in the Orthodox Old Testament; Psalm 51 in the Hebrew text):

> Have mercy on me, O God, in accordance with your great mercy. According to the multitude of your compassion blot out my offence. Wash me thoroughly from my wickedness, and cleanse me from my sin. For I acknowledge my wickedness, and my sin is ever before me. Against you alone I have sinned and done what is evil in your sight, that you may be justified in your words and win when you are judged. For see, in wickedness I was conceived and in sin my mother bore me. For see, you have loved truth; you have shown me the hidden and

▼

▶ The Orthodox Old Testament is the Ancient Greek translation known as the Septuagint (LXX). It was translated in stages between the third and second centuries BC and was used by the Jews of the Dispersion. It has been the Christian Old Testament since the first century AD. The numbering of the psalms diverges after Psalm 8 and reconverges from Psalm 148, as follows:

Septuagint	Hebrew
1–8	1–8
9	9–10
10–112	11–113
113	114–115
114	116 vv. 1–9
115	116 vv. 10–19
116–145	117–146
146	147 vv. 1–11
147	147 vv. 12–20
148–150	148–150
151*	

* Though contained in the earliest manuscripts of the Septuagint, Psalm 151 is not regarded as equal to the other 150 psalms; designated as "outside the number," it is never read in church.

secret things of your wisdom. You will sprinkle me with hyssop and I shall be cleansed. You will wash me and I shall be made whiter than snow. You will make me hear of joy and gladness; the bones which have been humbled will rejoice. Turn away your face from my sins and blot out all my iniquities. Create a clean heart in me, O God, and renew a right Spirit within me. Do not cast me out from your presence, and do not take your Holy Spirit from me. Give me back the joy of your salvation, and establish me with your sovereign Spirit. I will teach transgressors your ways, and sinners will turn to you again. O God, the God of my salvation, deliver me from bloodshed and my tongue will rejoice at your justice. Lord, you will open my lips, and my mouth will proclaim your praise. For if you had wanted a sacrifice, I would have given it. You will not take pleasure in burnt offerings. A sacrifice to God is a broken spirit; a broken and a humbled heart God will not despise. Do good to Sion, Lord, in your good pleasure; and let the walls of Jerusalem be rebuilt. Then you will be well pleased with a sacrifice of righteousness, oblation and whole burnt offerings. Then they will offer calves upon your altar. (EL)

During the Cherubic Hymn, just before the Great Entrance, when the gifts of bread and wine are brought to the altar, the priest censes the altar, the icons, and the people, and he quietly recites the psalm (and is expected to know it by heart). He recites the psalm up until verse 17: "A sacrifice to God is a broken spirit; a broken and a humbled heart God will not despise," and then concludes it after the solemn procession with the Holy Gifts when he places the bread and wine upon the altar: "Do good to Sion, Lord, in your good pleasure; and let the walls of Jerusalem be rebuilt. Then you will be well pleased with a sacrifice of righteousness, oblation and whole burnt offerings. Then they will offer calves upon your altar."

Psalm 50 was written by King David after he acknowledged and confessed his sin before the Prophet Nathan (2 Samuel[21] 12). David's sin was a terrible, twofold sin. He committed adultery with Bathsheba, the wife of Uriah the Hittite. Bathsheba became pregnant, and David sent for Uriah, who was with the Israelite army at the siege of Rabbah, so that he would make love to his wife and conceal the identity of the child's father. Uriah refused to abandon his companions on the field of battle, and so David sent him back to Joab, the commander, with a message instructing him to "put Uriah in the front line where the fighting is fiercest. Then withdraw from him so he will be struck down and die" (2 Kingdoms [2 Samuel] 11:15, VP).

Imagine: it is the prayer of a murderer and adulterer that the celebrant of the Liturgy recites (and makes his own in prayer) as he prepares to offer the bread and wine of the Eucharist at the Liturgy. The priest

7. *Bishop censing at the Cherubic Hymn*

is here expected to identify himself with a murderer and adulterer. But in so doing, he remembers also that David was not only forgiven but also chosen by God. Through repentance, he attained sanctity.

....

While the priest recites the psalm, the choir chants the Cherubic Hymn: "We who in a mystery represent the cherubim and sing the thrice-holy hymn to the life-giving Trinity, let us now lay aside every care of this life. For we are about to receive the King of all." In laying aside our worldly concerns, we are also to lay down before God our sins, to "cast our troubles on the Lord" (cf. Ps. 54:22 [55:22]), and having thus unburdened our hearts we may offer the Holy Oblation in peace. Indeed, this is what David did: "He went into the house of the Lord and worshiped" (2 Kingdoms [2 Samuel] 12:20, NKJV). Having identified ourselves with David's sinfulness, we imitate his repentance.

The Holy Oblation is offered not by the clergy alone but by the whole congregation. But it is the priest's particular cross to bear, his special calling and service to the Church, to take on the sins of the people as his own and to bring them before God and ask for His mercy. This is made clear in the prayers of the clergy at the Divine Liturgy: "Enable us to offer you gifts and spiritual sacrifices for our sins and those committed in ignorance by the people."

At the Great Entrance, we are not far from hearing the hymn of the Seraphim, which the Prophet Isaiah and the

> ▶ In Scripture, incense is a symbol of prayer: "Let my prayer arise in your sight as incense" (Ps. 140:2 [141:2], VP). "And the smoke of the incense, with the prayers of the saints, rose before God from the hand of the angel" (Rev. 8:4, ESV).
>
> But the act of censing is also a sign of veneration: "Everywhere a sacrifice of incense is offered to my name" (Mal. 1:11, VP).
>
> At the Divine Liturgy, the clergy cense the Holy Gifts, the icons, and also the people. This illustrates the profound respect the Orthodox Church has for the human person, made in the Image of God. The greatest icon is the human being.

beloved disciple John heard (Isa. 6:1; Rev. 4:8): "Holy, holy, holy, Lord Sabaoth; heaven and earth are full of your glory" (EL). And our response to this holiness is that of Isaiah: "Woe to me! . . . I am ruined! For I am a man of unclean lips, and I live among a people of unclean lips, and my eyes have seen the King, the LORD Almighty" (Isa. 6:5, NIV).

Our sense of sinfulness does not come from measuring the distance between our conduct and some sort of morality or law; it is only in the presence of God Himself, the only Holy One that we come to know how sinful we are. Is it not amazing that we are still permitted to come so close to Him! Indeed, in those moments we too may feel like murderers and adulterers. For the deeper we enter into the infinite holiness and presence of God, the more sinful we feel by comparison.

The psalm is not merely an expression of penitence and self-disgust. It is the overwhelming holiness of God that is the source of profound repentance, and it is particularly related to the coming of the Holy Spirit. The recitation of Psalm 50 is a preparation for the epiclesis, when we call on the Holy Spirit to change the bread and wine into Christ's Body and Blood. And so in Psalm 50 the priest says, "Create a clean heart in me, O God, and renew a right Spirit within me. Do not cast me out from your presence, and do not take your Holy Spirit from me." In the Liturgy of St. Basil the Great, the clergy pray that, despite their sins, the "Holy Spirit may come upon us and upon these gifts here set forth."

It is because of this sense of being in the presence of holiness that Psalm 50 is far from being pessimistic and melancholic. We are reminded that repentance finds its fulfillment not in looking back on our sins in despair but in looking forward with hope and faith; not in looking down into the pits of hell but in looking up to God in heaven. We are called to become what God wants us to be: holy. God says to His people: "Be holy, for I am holy" (Lev. 11:44, ESV). And St. Peter writes, "Just as he who called you is holy, so be holy in all you do" (1 Pet. 1:15, NIV).

▶ *Sabaoth* is a Hebrew word meaning "hosts" or "armies."
It is one of the few Hebrew words that the Greek Fathers
hardly ever translate into Greek. It is a title of majesty used
almost exclusively in connection with the name of God:
"Lord of Hosts."

Psalm 50 is a prayer not of despair but of hope: "You
will sprinkle me with hyssop and I shall be cleansed.
You will wash me and I shall be made whiter than snow.
You will make me hear of joy and gladness; the bones
which have been humbled will rejoice. . . . Give me
back the joy of your salvation, and establish me with
your sovereign Spirit. I will teach transgressors your
ways, and sinners will turn to you again." And we are
reminded that God hears the prayer and contrition of
the heart: "If you had wanted a sacrifice, I would have
given it. You will not take pleasure in burnt offerings.
A sacrifice to God is a broken spirit; a broken and a
humbled heart God will not despise."

Thus, as the Liturgy of the Faithful begins, we are
to unburden our hearts in confession before God as
we lay aside every care of this life, that we may "stand
with awe . . . stand with fear" and "pay heed to the Holy
Oblation, that in peace we may offer: mercy, peace: a
sacrifice of praise."

This is why the celebrant of the Liturgy, identifying himself with the worst of sinners, prays for God's mercy for himself and for the people as the Church begins to prepare for the Holy Oblation and to receive Christ in Holy Communion: "Wash me thoroughly from my wickedness, and cleanse me from my sin. . . . Turn away your face from my sins and blot out all my iniquities. Create a clean heart in me, O God, and renew a right Spirit within me." For only when we are at peace—with God, with one another, and with ourselves—can we worthily offer our liturgy to God and, in so doing, be made worthy to receive the Body and Blood of Christ for the forgiveness of sins and eternal life. Then "we will hear of joy and gladness; the bones which have been humbled will rejoice," and we can return to the world to "tell what great things God has done for us" (Luke 8:39, VP). And being thus filled with that divine joy and gladness, we can "teach transgressors your ways, and sinners will turn to you again."

❖ 8 ❖

Preparing for Holy Communion

Partaking of the divine mysteries is called Communion because it bestows on us unity with Christ and makes us partakers of His Kingdom.
—ST. ISIDORE OF PELUSIUM

Holy Communion is not something we rush into. We pray before we receive it. And so after the Holy Gifts have been placed on the altar, we begin what is called the Litany of the Precious Gifts.

> Let us complete our prayer to the Lord.
> For the precious gifts here set forth, let us pray to the Lord.

The Precious Gifts are the bread and wine that will become Holy Communion. We are going to receive Christ Himself within our very bodies! We are thus

8. *Holy Altar*

reminded that each of us is truly a temple of God. This is why it is so important to pray and prepare to receive Communion. People go to great pains to make sure that their house is clean and tidy before receiving a guest. How much more should we prepare the house of the soul to receive Christ!

Receiving Communion

But what must Orthodox Christians do to receive Communion? There are many misunderstandings about this issue. The first is summed up well by Fr. Alexander Schmemann:

In many Orthodox Churches there developed, and is commonly accepted today, the doctrine which affirms that Communion for laity is impossible without sacramental confession and absolution. Even if someone wishes to receive Communion frequently, he must each time go to confession or at least receive sacramental absolution.

The time has come to state openly that whatever the various and sometimes serious reasons that brought this doctrine and this practice into existence, they not only have no foundation in Tradition, but, in fact, lead to very alarming distortions of the Orthodox doctrine of the

Church, of the Eucharist, and of the Sacrament
of Penance itself.[22]

While Schmemann is writing of the Russian
Tradition, it is true that in general we have sometimes
tended to see "participation" in the Liturgy as one
thing and Communion as something else, something
"extra." This rationale has been pushed so far that we
have placed endless boundaries and hurdles on the
layperson's path to Communion.

What are these obstacles to coming to Holy
Communion? The first is Confession, the second is the
Prayers of Preparation for Holy Communion, and the
third is fasting for a period of time from certain foods.

St. John Chrysostom once said this about how all of
us prepare for Holy Communion:

> There are cases when a priest does not differ
> from a layman, notably when one approaches
> the Holy Mysteries. We are all equally given
> them, not as in the Old Testament when one
> food was for the priests and another for the
> people and when it was not permitted to the
> people to partake of that which was for the
> priest. Now it is not so: but to all is offered the
> same Body and the same Cup.[23]

In other words, when it comes to Holy Communion, there is no distinction between clergy and laity. Whatever preparation is required of the one is required of the other. It therefore seems remarkable that some clergy insist that the laity must go to Confession every time they are to take Communion. How many clergy, I wonder, go to Confession before every Liturgy they celebrate? The decline of Confession in many places is lamentable, and the Sacrament of Repentance and Reconciliation certainly needs to be explained and encouraged (not only to those who never or hardly ever go to Confession but also to those who see it as something mechanical, as though regular Confession—with or without genuine repentance—makes us "worthy" of Holy Communion). But this "rule" that Confession must precede Communion seems tantamount to supposing that Communion is the "obligation" of the clergy but not of the laity.

Furthermore, the insistence on Sacramental Confession prior to Communion seems to display a complete ignorance of the most conspicuous and well-known words of the Holy Oblation: "This is my body . . . this is my blood . . . *for the forgiveness of sins.*" If we truly believe that the Body and Blood of Christ is for the forgiveness of sins, why is it that we require forgiveness of sins in Sacramental Confession or in the prayer of "absolution" before receiving it?

The invitation for all Orthodox Christians to receive Communion, regardless of their failings and shortcomings, is made most explicit at Easter, in the beautiful Paschal Homily of St. John Chrysostom:

> The Lord is generous and receives the last as the first. . . . He has pity on the latter, he cares for the former. He gives to the one, he is generous to the other. He accepts the work done, he welcomes the intention. He honours the achievement, he praises the purpose. Therefore all of you enter into the joy of our Lord. . . . The table is full, all of you enjoy yourselves. The calf is fatted, let none go away hungry. All of you enjoy the banquet of the faith. All of you enjoy the richness of his goodness. Let no one grieve at their poverty: for the kingdom of all has been revealed. Let no one bewail their faults: for forgiveness has risen from the tomb. (EL)

A second obstacle that has been placed in the way of many to come to the Lord's Table is what are often called Prayers of Preparation for Communion, or lengthy prayers found in our Orthodox prayer books, and which some believe must be recited the night before or in the morning before coming to church if they are to receive Communion. The idea that the Liturgy itself—its very goal and purpose being participation in the divine Mysteries—constitutes the preparation before and the thanksgiving after Holy Communion does not seem to occur to us. I hope that it has already become clear, and if not, that it will do as I continue to explain the Liturgy, that the prayers, hymns, and petitions of the Liturgy itself are precisely to prepare us for Communion. Nearly all the petitions and prayers from the Cherubic Hymn onward (the Liturgy of the Faithful) are made with the purpose of preparing us. Likewise, all the prayers of the Divine Liturgy following participation in the Holy Gifts are made with the purpose of giving thanks for Communion. There is, of course, nothing wrong with Christians saying additional prayers of preparation at home, if they so choose, but I think it is a mistake to make this an obligation for everyone.

There is also, then, what is often a third obstacle to people coming to partake of Holy Communion: fasting. There seems to be confusion between "complete abstinence" before Communion and "ascetic fasting" (abstinence from certain foods). Let me explain. In the Orthodox Church, there is a great deal of ascetic fasting. During Lent, Advent, and some other periods of the year, not to mention almost every Wednesday and Friday, we abstain from meat and dairy. These days and periods of fasting are not related to receiving Communion. Whether we receive Communion or not, Orthodox Christians are expected to observe these fasts. The only kind of fasting that Orthodoxy has established for the purpose of receiving Communion is a complete abstinence from all food and drink on the morning that Communion is to be taken, or from the afternoon if we are to receive Communion at the evening liturgies held during Lent. The idea of abstaining from certain foods for a day or several days before Communion seems to have no basis in our Tradition.

Finally, we must avoid the age-old error of avoiding Communion because we think we are too sinful to receive it. The Eucharist is not a reward for good behavior; it is granted to us for the forgiveness of sins and eternal life. As St. John Cassian put it, and which is a good note to end on,

> We must not avoid communion because we deem ourselves to be sinful. We must approach it more often for the healing of the soul and the purification of the spirit, but with such humility and faith that considering ourselves unworthy . . . we should more greatly desire the medicine of our wounds. Otherwise it is impossible to receive communion once a year, as certain people do . . . considering the sanctification of heavenly Mysteries as available only to saints. It is better to think that by giving us grace, the sacrament makes us pure and holy. Such people

manifest more pride than humility . . . for when they receive, they think themselves as worthy. It is much better if, in humility of heart, knowing that we are never worthy of the Holy Mysteries we would receive them every Sunday for the healing of our diseases, rather than, blinded by pride, think that after one year we become worthy of receiving them.[24]

▶ People who are unable to fast—such as those who need to take medication in the mornings, women who are pregnant or breastfeeding, and other such cases—are not expected to fast at all before Communion. Fasting has never been imposed on those who are not healthy enough for it. Those who need to eat in the morning in order to take medication, for example, should not avoid Communion because of this.

9. *The Litany of the Precious Gifts*

9

The Litany of the Precious Gifts

Prayer is the fruit of joy and thankfulness.
—ABBA EVAGRIUS

The Litany of the Precious Gifts continues: "That the whole day may be perfect, holy, peaceful and sinless, let us ask of the Lord." What does this mean? Are we meant to take it literally?

Ideally, we would always carry with us from the church out into the world the joyful experience of God's holy love and presence. Even if it is for just a short while, our inner selves and therefore our very lives, our conversations, our activities, would be imbued with the quiet joy and silent radiance of the Divine Liturgy. When the Liturgy ends, we are dismissed from the church. We are sent back out into the world. People would see us leaving the church and wonder what it is they are missing out on.

But, of course, that does not often happen, does it? Instead we leave the church mostly unchanged. It is not that the Liturgy is inadequate; it is because we do not pray as we should. We should be silent and prayerful during the Divine Liturgy. For it is only by silencing ourselves, not only physically, but also inwardly, that we can hear the still and gentle voice of the Holy Spirit within us. The Liturgy is a time for us to come face-to-face with God and to be inwardly changed from that divine encounter; that change will affect the course of the day. Then, ideally—and I think it is possible—the whole day, and not just an hour or so, may be perfect, holy, peaceful, and sinless.

We ask for "an angel of peace, a faithful guide, a guardian of our souls and bodies." Every Orthodox Christian has a guardian angel who watches over him, guides him, and prays for him. There is even a prayer to one's guardian angel, which many Orthodox say as part of their evening prayers at home. Such an angel may guide us and protect us in our lives. Being fallen human beings, we need the help of the heavenly hosts, of the angels and saints. We ask them to intercede to Christ on our behalf, as they are ever standing before God.

We ask for "pardon and forgiveness of our sins and offences," and we ask "that we may live out the rest of our days in peace and repentance." Peace, that is spiritual peace, "the peace of God that surpasses all understanding" (Phil. 4:7, VP), goes hand in hand with repentance. For as long as we are at odds with God and with our own conscience, we will not be at peace, and so we must reconcile ourselves with God. But we cannot do that until we realize that we are in the wrong, that we are not doing what God wants us to do, that we are not what God wants us to be. Repentance is ultimately the act of admitting we are in the wrong and saying sorry; it is the pursuit of God's forgiveness.

To repent literally means to have a change of heart, or to change one's mind, and we constantly need to have this change of heart and mind because we do not think as God thinks; we do not desire what God desires. In the Old Testament, God says to the people of Israel, "My thoughts are not your thoughts, neither are your ways my ways" (Isa. 55:8, NIV). This repentance does not happen overnight—it is a way of life, a life in which we are constantly striving to better ourselves, to become more like God, to think more like Him, to love what He loves, to desire what He desires. Therefore we ask "that we may live out the rest of our days in peace and repentance."

▶ In the Litany of the Precious Gifts, the usual response of the people, "Lord, have mercy," is replaced by the words, "Grant this, O Lord." Again, we see the principle of keeping our words to a bare minimum, for the reasons laid out in chapter 2.

We ask for "those things which are good and profitable for our souls." It is for such things that we should pray. So many people are confused and angered when their prayers are not answered. But we must ask ourselves, do we ask for the right things? And do we ask for them rightly?

Children often plead with their parents to give them something they want, and the mother or father knows that what the child wants is no good for them, and they refuse, and the child starts screaming and crying and claiming that "it's not fair!" How little we change when we grow up! We are often like little children, asking God for this and that, and God knows full well that what we are asking for is not right for us, even if we cannot understand why. We must learn to trust in God's wisdom and judgment. But also, we should ask ourselves, do we ask rightly, and do we actually deserve what we ask for?

If your child is rude and ungrateful, and is demanding, "Give me this! Give me that!" or if the child himself is selfish and unkind to his brother or sister, do you not refuse until the child learns manners, generosity, fairness? Are we not the same? We may say, "God, help me," the minute after we have refused to help a fellow human being. We may say, "God, forgive me," just after we have refused to forgive someone who has asked us to pardon them. If God does not answer our prayers, we should know that there is always good reason for it, and we cannot always know the reason. We cannot see into the future; we cannot see the long-term consequences of our actions or of any given situation—but God does. So we pray only for "those things which are good and profitable for our souls," and sometimes what is good for us is not very pleasant!

We pray for "a Christian end to our life, painless, unashamed and peaceful, and for a good defence before the dread judgement seat of Christ." We are reminded that Christ will come again as judge, and we will all stand before His judgment seat. We will be called to account for our lives, our actions, our words. And so we ask for a Christian end to our life. In other words, we ask that we may be found to be faithful until the end. But if we want to die like Christians, we must live like Christians. None of us knows when death will come upon us; we must always be ready for it. And the only way to be always ready for it is to live a life of perpetual repentance; a life in which we humble ourselves before God; in which we struggle to learn love and forgiveness, patience, and goodness; a life that does not live for itself but that finds its fulfillment and joy in God and His Kingdom.

Christ tells us that the Kingdom of God is like a pearl of enormous value. When someone finds it and realizes its worth, he sells everything he has in order to obtain that pearl (Matt. 13:45–46). At the Divine Liturgy, we are reminded that what is more important than anything in this world, more valuable than anything in life, more precious than life itself, is the Kingdom of God. If we sacrifice everything for that Kingdom, we will find that we have not really sacrificed anything at all, but rather, we will have gained something more precious than anything in the world. We will have gained eternal life, the life of God and His Kingdom, which shall have no end.

❖ 10 ❖

The Creed:
Holy Trinity

*The Kingdom of God is knowledge
of the Holy Trinity.*
—ABBA EVAGRIUS

After the Litany of the Precious Gifts, before we say the Creed, the priest turns to face the people and blesses them, saying "Peace to all." Then we hear the command, "Let us love one another that with one mind we may confess: Father, Son and Holy Spirit, Trinity consubstantial and undivided."

It is significant that we hear this command just before we begin to recite the Creed because in the Church, there is no discrepancy between dogma and love, between faith and works. As St. John the Evangelist writes, "Whoever says 'I love God' and hates his brother is a liar" (1 John 4:20, VP). We cannot truly confess our belief in God if we do not first love one another.

The Creed is introduced with another proclamation made by the deacon: "The doors! The doors! With wisdom let us attend." What is the meaning of this proclamation, "The doors! The doors!"?

▶ When there is more than one priest celebrating the Liturgy, we sing: "Let us love one another that with one mind we may confess: I will love you, Lord, my strength. The Lord is my firm foundation, my refuge and my deliverer."

This proclamation has been preserved from ancient times, when the doors of the church were jealously guarded and only members of the Church could attend the Divine Liturgy. The proclamation "The doors! The doors!" was a command to the doorkeepers of the church to ensure that no one would enter the church from this point. The Liturgy is not a public thing, but one of the mysteries of the faith. That faith is summed up in the Creed, and those who do not believe in the Creed could not participate in the Church's Liturgy.

Of course, the Church today is far more open to outsiders, and it does not prohibit anyone from attending the Liturgy, though it does not grant Communion to anyone who is not a baptized Orthodox Christian. So this command, "The doors! The doors!" is only really of historic interest, though it does serve as a reminder that any Orthodox Christian who is to participate in Communion should be in church before the Creed at the very latest. But we cannot receive

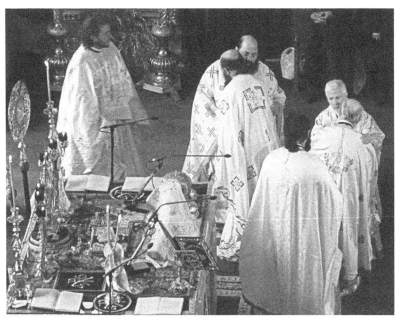

10. *The clergy giving one another the Kiss of Peace before the Creed*
("Let us love one another ...")

Communion in the Church unless we accept the Church's doctrines. Thus at every Divine Liturgy we together reaffirm and profess our faith in the Creed, which all Christians should know by heart:

I believe in one God, Father, Almighty, maker of heaven and earth, of all things visible and invisible.

And in one Lord Jesus Christ, the only-begotten Son of God, begotten from the Father before all ages. Light from Light, true God from true God, begotten not made, consubstantial with the Father; through him all things were made; for our sake and for our salvation he came down from heaven, and was incarnate from the Holy Spirit and the Virgin Mary and became man; he was crucified also for us under Pontius Pilate, and suffered and was buried; he rose again on the third day, in accordance with the Scriptures, and ascended into heaven and is seated at the right hand of the Father; he is coming again in glory to judge the living and the dead; and his kingdom will have no end.

And in the Holy Spirit, the Lord, the Giver of life, who proceeds from the Father, who together with Father and Son is worshipped and together glorified; who spoke through the Prophets. In one, Holy, Catholic and Apostolic

Church; I confess one Baptism for the forgiveness of sins. I await the resurrection of the dead
and the life of the age to come. Amen.

It is worth noting that we say, "I believe," not "we
believe." The reason is that the Creed was originally and
still is a baptismal creed. It is the creed that is said before
our baptism. Communion is the renewal and confirmation
of that baptism, of our membership in the Church. This
is why only those who are baptized Orthodox can receive
Holy Communion in the Orthodox Church. And this is
why the Creed is recited before we receive Communion.
Holy Communion does not create Christian unity; it is
the result of Christian unity.

In the Creed we confess our belief in one God: the
Father, Jesus Christ, and the Holy Spirit. Christianity,
along with the other monotheistic faiths, believes in
one God. But unlike Judaism and Islam, this oneness
does not exclude a plurality of persons in the Godhead.
If you ask a Jew or Muslim, "Who is God?" their answer
may be a variety of names for God, but all of them
would be the equivalent of what Christians know as the
Father. For the Christian, this is only part of the truth,
and does not reveal the fullness of the Godhead.

If you ask a Christian, "What is God?" he would
probably respond with the words of St. John the
Evangelist, and say, "God is love" (1 John 4:8), and
God is love because God is more than one person.

Only a person can love. Many like to think of God as an impersonal, mystical force, but then we cannot speak of a God who loves and forgives—only a person can love and forgive. Also, true love is not self-love. True love is the love of another, of someone or something outside ourselves. Love must have an object—it cannot exist without more than one person. God is love because He is Trinity: three persons in one Godhead, in an eternal relationship of love. This is why our profession of faith in the Trinity is introduced with the words, "Let us love one another that with one mind we may confess: Father, Son and Holy Spirit, Trinity consubstantial and undivided." For only by loving one another can we make a true confession of faith in the Trinity.

After we profess our belief in the "Father, Almighty, Maker of heaven and earth and of all things visible and invisible," we confess our belief in "one Lord Jesus Christ, the only-begotten Son of God, begotten of the Father before all ages. Light from Light, true God from true God, begotten, not made, consubstantial with the Father. Through Him all things were made."

The Church holds that Christ always existed. As one of the Trinity, there was never a time that He was not in existence. While subject to the Father, Who is the head and source of the Son and Holy Spirit, He is eternally "begotten" of the Father, but "not made," not a created being. Thus we declare that He is "consubstantial" (of one essence) with the Father.

While the Son and Spirit have their source and origin in the Father, they are all equally God. There is one God because there is one source: the Father. The Son is eternally begotten of the Father; the Spirit eternally proceeds from the Father. This does not mean that the Son and Spirit were created by the Father. Rather, it describes an eternal relationship between the persons of the Trinity.

As the Church, we are called to acquire the relationship of love and unity we find in the Trinity. At His Last Supper, our Lord prayed that we may all be one, as He and the Father are one (John 17:21). The Church is a paradigm of the Trinity: different persons, but one body. Thus only when there is love and unity between us can we make a true confession of faith in God the Trinity: "Let us love one another that with one mind we may confess: Father, Son and Holy Spirit, Trinity consubstantial and undivided."

▶ The word *consubstantial* (In Greek, *homoousios*) is one of the most important words in Christian theology (and, at the same time, one of the most incomprehensible). With this word, the Church explains how three persons constitute one God and not three gods. Since the three persons of the Trinity are of the same *ousia*—the same *essence*, or *substance*—they are one.

11. *Dome with Icon of Christ the Almighty (Pantocrator)*

❧ 11 ❧
The Creed: Jesus Christ

*Where there are two or three gathered in my name,
there I am in the midst of them.*
—MATT. 18:20, VP

Until now we have been speaking of Christ as God before the creation of the universe, as coeternal with the Father, true God from true God. Through Him all things were made. All things were created by the Trinity, and that includes the "Only-begotten Son and Word of God," Jesus Christ.

Then we proclaim our belief in the Incarnation, the doctrine of God become a man:

> For our sake and for our salvation, he came down from heaven, and was incarnate from the Holy Spirit and the Virgin Mary, and became man.

The second person of the Trinity, the Son and Word of God, became flesh and blood like us and lived among us. Divine and human nature were united in Him. Since God has shared in our mortal and carnal nature, so too now can we share in His immortal and divine nature.

But why did God become man? Humanity was made in the Image of the Trinity, Who is the ultimate image of love. God is love because He is Trinity. But if God is love, then He is also freedom, for love can only be freely given. Therefore, humans were free to reject God's love and take their own path. This they did, as we read in Genesis. It is known as the fall of humanity, or the ancestral sin. Humans disobeyed God's will, and thus all that was contrary to God entered into human life and creation. Thus death (an opposite of God—for God is life) entered the world, and humanity was no longer able to attain the likeness of God, the likeness of divinity and immortality. So God took the initiative. Since humans could not obtain the likeness of God, God took on the likeness of man. He became a part of His creation, a human being. Jesus Christ is the second person of the Trinity become a man. His becoming a human being like us, His Incarnation, would not have been possible without the Virgin Mary, and therefore we venerate her as the "Mother of God" (*Theotokos*). Christ is without mother in divinity, without father in humanity, but His divine and human natures are combined in one person, the person of Jesus Christ. Since she gave birth to God in the flesh, we revere the Virgin Mary as Mother of God.

We then proclaim our belief in the passion, death, resurrection, and ascension of Christ:

> He was crucified also for us under Pontius Pilate. He suffered and was buried. On the third day he rose again in accordance with the Scriptures, and ascended into heaven, and is seated at the right hand of the Father.

The whole point of Christ becoming a man is to restore humankind's relationship with God. Christ is both God and man at once, and so it is only through Him that this restoration can happen. Christ, therefore, had to undergo everything that we do; and one thing that we all undergo without exception is death. Whatever Christ has done, whatever He has taken on and made His own, has been made holy by virtue of His divinity—a way to salvation.

In effect, Christ paved a road for us. It is the same road that we have always trodden, the one that begins at birth and ends at death. But God cannot die, unless He becomes mortal like us, subject to death. So in Christ we have this paradox: mortal and yet eternal, human and yet divine. Since God is the source of life, and death has no power over Him, death was destroyed by the death of God. This is why, at Easter (Pascha), we sing again and again of Christ's Resurrection, "by death he has trampled on death."

The birth, suffering, crucifixion, death, resurrection, and ascension of Christ were all foretold in the Scriptures (the Old Testament). "He rose again on the third day in accordance with the Scriptures." It was, since the dawn of time, God's plan for our salvation.

By His blood our sins are washed away. Christ, having become one of us, part of the human race, is able on our behalf to atone for our sins, to offer Himself up for all of us. Being the only human being without sin, and voluntarily sacrificing Himself, His sacrifice is the only perfect sacrifice.

Being the Son of the heavenly Father, Christ is able to destroy death and refashion our mortal nature and to take it up to God in heaven. Herein lies the importance of Christ's ascension and sitting at the right hand of the Father. Christ did not leave His human body and nature behind in the Resurrection. He raised it up with Him, and so took humanity up into the heights of heaven to God the Father. Therefore, death is no longer the end of human life. For this reason, when we speak of the departed in the Church, we speak not of "death" (*thanatos*) but of "sleep" (*koimesis*). When we go to sleep, we all expect that we shall wake up. So too, when we die, we Christians expect that we shall rise again. Christ has vanquished the power of death, and God shall raise us all up at the last day.

We then profess our belief in Christ's Second
Coming:

He is coming again in glory to judge the
living and the dead, and his kingdom will have
no end.

The Church believes that Christ will come again to
judge the world. His second coming will not be like the
first. In the Gospels, Christ Himself describes His Second
Coming: "Then the sign of the Son of Man will appear in
heaven, and then all the tribes of the earth will mourn,
and they will see the Son of Man coming on the clouds
of heaven with power and great glory. And He will send
His angels with a great sound of a trumpet, and they will
gather together His elect from the four winds, from one
end of heaven to the other" (Matt. 24:30–31, NKJV).

▶ God's plan for our salvation is what is called "divine economy." This theological term, *economy* (Greek, *oikonomia*),
means the "handling" or "disposition" or "management" of
something. The divine economy is therefore God's handling
or management of a world and a human race that has fallen
away from God. At the heart of this divine economy is the
sacrifice made on behalf of all humanity by the Son of God.

Christ will not come again in humility and in secret. He will come from above in glory, and every eye shall see Him. That is why Christ warns us,

> If anyone says to you, "Look, here *is* the Christ!" or "There!" do not believe *it.* For false christs and false prophets will rise and show great signs and wonders to deceive, if possible, even the elect. See, I have told you beforehand. Therefore if they say to you, "Look, He is in the desert!" do not go out; *or* "Look, *He is* in the inner rooms!" do not believe *it.* For as the lightning comes from the east and flashes to the west, so also will the coming of the Son of Man be. (Matt. 24:23–27, NKJV)

Christ will come to judge the living and the dead. He will judge everyone according to their works. One of the most famous passages on this Last Judgment is found, like the passages we have just been looking at, in Matthew's Gospel (25:31–46), when we hear Christ judge us according to whether we have fed, clothed, and visited the needy:

> Come, you who are blessed by my Father, inherit the kingdom prepared for you from the foundation of the world. For I was hungry and you gave me food, I was thirsty and you gave me

drink, I was a stranger and you welcomed me, I was naked and you clothed me, I was sick and you visited me, I was in prison and you came to me. . . . Truly, I say to you, as you did it to one of the least of these my brothers, you did it to me. (ESV)

We will be judged above all by love, and the love by which we will be judged is not some general, abstract love for humanity, not some sentimental and optimistic outlook on human nature, but love toward specific human beings. There is nothing abstract or sentimental about Christian love. Christian love is made manifest in concrete actions. It is experienced and manifested in sacrifice, in charity, in forgiveness, in prayer, in humility. Love is not just for sentimental optimists. In fact, one of the great distortions in people's understanding of love is its confusion with sentimentality. Real love requires strength of spirit, courage, sacrifice. Sentimentality, abstract love for humanity, demands nothing but idealistic speculation.

Thus we are reminded that we will be judged above all by God's love, by whether we have carried out the two great commandments: love God and love your neighbor. The Gospel passage of the Last Judgment reminds us that we cannot do the one without the other. And this is revealed quite plainly in the word "I": *I* was hungry, *I* was thirsty, *I* was a stranger, *I* was sick, *I* was a prisoner. In every person we see Christ, the "Image" of God. For every human being is an icon of Christ. If we show love to one another, we show love to Christ Himself.

Let us therefore learn to really love one another—let us give to the needy, visit those who are sick or lonely, welcome strangers—so that when we are finally standing before Christ at the Last Judgment, we will be standing before someone whom we have truly loved.

❖ 12 ❖
The Creed:
Holy Spirit

*The Spirit himself will concelebrate
with us all the days of our life.*
—LITURGY OF ST. JOHN CHRYSOSTOM

A t this point, as we continue to say the Creed, we enter into one of the most mysterious aspects of our faith. We say, I believe

in the Holy Spirit, the Lord, the Giver of life, who proceeds from the Father, who together with Father and Son is worshipped and together glorified, who spoke through the Prophets.

The Holy Spirit is one of the most difficult areas of theology to explain. Even the Creed itself, originally, barely made mention of Him. It was only after the divinity of the Holy Spirit was called into question in the fourth century that the Church, and in particular

12. *The clergy holding the veil over the Holy Gifts*
during the recitation of the Creed

St. Basil the Great, began to formulate a clearer position on the Holy Spirit.

This passage from the Creed was added because there were Christians who began to argue that the Holy Spirit was not God in the sense that the Father and the Son are God. Thus the Creed explicitly states that the Holy Spirit is called Lord, just as Father and Son are, that He is the giver of life, and that He is worshiped and glorified together with the Father and Son.

God is known in three persons; He is, in other words, a "personal" God, which means that we can have a personal relationship with Him. I reiterate this because the term *Spirit* can lead us to forget that the third person of the Trinity is also a *person* of the Trinity in the same sense that Father and Son are persons. The Holy Spirit is therefore not to be understood as an impersonal force but as someone we have a relationship with. As God is love, He is also freedom, because love can only be freely given. Often in Scripture we hear of people, particularly the Prophets and Apostles, being "filled with the Holy Spirit." But the Holy Spirit is a spirit of freedom. He is not a Spirit that possesses us against our will. Thus it is characteristic that St. Seraphim of Sarov said that the whole purpose of Christian life is to *acquire* the Holy Spirit.

The Holy Spirit dwells within us. His grace and power comes upon everyone who is anointed in baptism. He reveals to us all truth, as our Lord promised He would at His Last Supper: "But when he, the Spirit of truth, comes, he will guide you into all truth" (John 16:13, NIV). The Holy Spirit resides in the Church and guides her. But, as I said already, He is a Spirit of freedom. Though He comes and dwells in us, we must also be willing for the Holy Spirit to work within us. But how can we recognize the Holy Spirit? What are the fruits of the Holy Spirit? St. Paul, in his First Epistle to the Galatians, writes: "The fruit of the Spirit is love, joy, peace, patience, kindness, goodness, faithfulness, gentleness, self-control" (Gal. 5:22–23, ESV).

There are some Christian groups who focus very strongly on the Holy Spirit. They display that they are filled with the Holy Spirit in ways that are often ecstatic. Often they will scream and shout, leap and dance, even faint. But according to Orthodox theology, these are not the signs of the Holy Spirit. As St. John writes in his first Epistle: "Do not believe every spirit, but test the spirits to see whether they are from God, for many false prophets have gone out into the world" (1 John 4:1, ESV). Instead, we believe that the Holy Spirit is recognized by the fruits that St. Paul mentions: "love, joy, peace, patience, kindness, goodness, faithfulness, gentleness, self-control."

This may be one reason why some Christians reject Orthodoxy as a stale, ritualistic religion that is void of the grace of the Holy Spirit. They think that we have abandoned the Holy Spirit for Tradition. But this is to misunderstand both us and our Tradition.

As the influential Russian theologian Vladimir Lossky succinctly wrote: "Tradition is the life of the Holy Spirit in the Church."[25] Tradition is the life of the past being lived in the present, and therefore it is always old yet new, ancient yet present. It connects us with the Christians of the early Church and with the Saints throughout the ages. It is indeed the life of the Holy Spirit in the Church, for it is the very same Tradition and therefore the same divinely inspired way of life that has been imparted to us from generation to generation since the time of the Apostles.

The Holy Spirit abides in the Church and guides her. But while we can be sure that the Holy Spirit is at work in the Church, we cannot say that He is not present or even that He is not active anywhere else. In the best-known Orthodox prayer to the Holy Spirit, we address Him as "present everywhere and filling all things." While the Holy Spirit dwells in the Church, He is not bound by it. As St. Maximus the Confessor wrote in the seventh century: "God is breath, and the breath of the wind is shared by all; nothing shuts it in, nothing holds it prisoner."[26]

13. *Church interior*

❖ 13 ❖

The Creed:
The Church

*No one can have God as his Father without
having the Church as his Mother.*
—St. Cyprian of Carthage

I believe "in one, Holy, Catholic and Apostolic Church." We make this proclamation of faith every time we recite the Creed at the Divine Liturgy.

But there is much confusion about the nature of the Church. *Church* is a word that is used a great deal, and yet those who employ the term are often not clear what they mean by it. The word *church* is used to refer to a building, and it is sometimes used to mean Christianity worldwide. But the Church is, at least from an Orthodox perspective, something more specific than Christendom.

The Church as the Kingdom of God

The Church is the Kingdom of God. Many Christians think of the Kingdom as something that is purely heavenly and that has not yet arrived on earth, while they see the Church as some sort of instrument for promulgating the Gospel, an earthly institution of believers. The Church is more than this. In the Church we have a foretaste of the Kingdom of Heaven. That which reveals the Church as the heavenly Kingdom is first and foremost our worship, and especially the Liturgy.

There is an overwhelming supernatural impression and heavenly beauty about the Divine Liturgy that is not accidental. The Liturgy of the Church is not merely the gathering of believers on earth but the gathering of heaven and earth together in one place. As we hear in the Cherubic Hymn of the Liturgy of the Presanctified Gifts: "Now the powers of heaven worship with us invisibly." And not only do the angels invisibly worship with us: Christ Himself comes to us again in a material form—as bread and wine—and is both spiritually and physically present with us. Heaven and earth, God and humankind, are gathered together in one place at the Divine Liturgy. Wherever Christ is, there is the Church. For the Church can have no true identity or fulfillment without its Head and Savior, Jesus Christ.

The Church Is One

Ultimately, there is only one Church. There is one Christ, and He has one Body.

St. Paul writes, "There is one body and one Spirit, just as you were called to one hope . . . one Lord, one faith, one baptism" (Eph. 4:4–5, NIV). But "oneness" has not only a numerical connotation—it also implies unity and union. This unity is first of all a unity of the individual members of the local church in faith and in Communion; it extends to the unity of its groups— parishes, dioceses—and beyond, across the different cultural and historical backgrounds of the Orthodox Churches throughout the world—Greek, Russian, Antiochene, Serbian, Bulgarian, Georgian, Romanian, and so on. The Church is one because it has one head: Christ. We are not to see the Church in geographical terms or in terms of numbers and statistics but in spiritual terms—in terms of its unity in Christ. Christian unity does not mean agreeing to disagree: on matters of theological truth, we must be of one mind if we are to share together in the Eucharist. Therefore the Orthodox Church strives to preserve its internal unity as something precious and essential to its spiritual and sacramental life.

The Church Is Holy

The Church is holy because Christ is holy. As St. Paul writes: "Christ loved the Church and gave himself for her, that he might sanctify her, having purified her with the washing of water with a word, that he might present the Church to himself glorious, without spot or wrinkle or anything similar, but that she might be holy and unblemished" (Eph. 5:25–27, EL). From the time we are received into the Church, whether as infants or as adults, we are called to become what we are, to become holy. God says to His people: "Be holy, for I am holy" (Lev. 11:44, ESV).

The Church Is Catholic

Catholic means "universal." It also means "complete." The Orthodox Church is Catholic in the sense that it is complete because it is the Body of Christ and the Holy Spirit fills it and guides it into all truth. It is Catholic in the sense that it is universal because it is for all people and all places. It is not just for Greeks, Slavs, and Arabs but is for people throughout the world. But it is Catholic also because it is for all times. Orthodox doctrine does not change with the times because universal truths remain true in every age, ancient and modern.

The Church Is Apostolic

When we say that the Church is Apostolic we intend that the Orthodox Church is founded upon the work and teaching of the Apostles, who were commanded by our Lord to "make disciples of all nations, baptizing them in the name of the Father and of the Son and of the Holy Spirit, teaching them to observe all that I have commanded you" (Matt. 28:19–20, ESV). The Apostles appointed bishops, priests, and deacons to continue their work and to serve the local churches, and those bishops in turn appointed other bishops, and those bishops did the same, and so on and so on, in a continued unbroken chain until today. This is what is called the "Apostolic Succession" of bishops. The perpetual celebration of the Eucharist, the continued proclamation of the unchanging message of the Gospel, the unbroken line of bishops: these three things are fundamental characteristics of the Church's Apostolicity.

Is There Salvation Outside the Church?

Some of the Church Fathers taught that "there is no salvation outside the Church." What does this mean?

This does not mean that only members of the Orthodox Church will be saved. Instead, it means this: there is no salvation outside the Church because the Church is the Kingdom of God. All who are saved at the end of time, since the beginning of creation until Christ's glorious coming again, will enter the Kingdom of God, which means they will be received into the Church of Christ. Salvation makes us members of the Church.

There is no salvation outside the Church because salvation *is* the Church. So not only is it untrue that those who are not Orthodox have no hope of salvation, but also, being Orthodox does not guarantee salvation. We will be judged each according to our ability, according to what we have been given, according to our works and measure of grace. I believe that the Orthodox Church is the one, Holy, Catholic, and Apostolic Church of which the Creed speaks. I believe that the Orthodox Church is the Kingdom of Heaven on earth. I can only hope that, when I come to stand before Christ at the Last Judgment, He will deem me worthy to still be a part of it.

⚜ 14 ⚜

The Creed:
Baptism

*Unless one is born again he cannot see
the kingdom of God.*
—JOHN 3:3, ESV

We are initiated into the Church by baptism. It is the greatest prerequisite for full participation in the Divine Liturgy. Every time we recite the Creed, we proclaim our belief in this ancient Sacrament, which was established by Christ Himself: "I accept one baptism for the forgiveness of sins."

For centuries, baptism was a part of the Easter Liturgy. The entire period of Lent leading to Holy Week and Easter was structured around the preparation of those who had come to believe in Christ but were being instructed in the Faith in order to eventually be baptized. These candidates for baptism were known as catechumens. Easter was the day when they were baptized and received into the Church in the presence

14. *Baptism ceremony*

of the whole congregation and would celebrate with them their "being buried with Christ by baptism unto death, so that as Christ was raised from the dead, so they too may walk in newness of life," as the Epistle Reading for baptism tells us. Easter was thus a baptismal liturgy, and baptism was the celebration of the new life of the Resurrection, which was given to those who were being incorporated into the Church through baptism.

This is not merely of historical interest: it reminds us of the true spirit and nature of baptism. The gradual transformation of baptism into a private affair for a specific family in some corner of the church makes it hard for a modern Christian to understand the authentic meaning of baptism—that of the incorporation of the baptized into the redeemed and sanctified Body of Christ, the spiritual family that is the Church in its fullness.

The baptism service today is divided into two parts, similar to the two parts of the Divine Liturgy. The first part is called the Service for the Making of a Catechumen, though most people today refer to it as the exorcisms. This service was originally completely separate from baptism. After a period of instruction, a person who desired to be baptized would be made a catechumen, someone being prepared for baptism, and would then continue to undergo instruction for a further one to three years before being baptized. The first half of the baptism service is the last surviving element of this long preparation.

In the first half of the baptism service, which usually takes place in the western end of the church, the priest or bishop prays over the candidate and recites several exorcisms. Then he questions the candidate three times: "Do you renounce Satan, and all his worship, and all his works, and all his solemn rites?" and the candidate replies each time, "I do renounce them."

It may seem strange to people nowadays that baptism begins with the renunciation of Satan. But becoming a Christian means entering into a spiritual war. Satan is a fallen angel who opposes God's will and opposes us. Therefore to embrace Christ, we must be liberated from Satan's tyranny and oppression, and we must take up arms against him.

The candidate is then turned around to face east. Traditionally, Orthodox Christians have always prayed eastward, and the altar is nearly always found on the east side of the Church. Praying toward the east is an ancient tradition that began with the Old Testament: "The prince should prepare a whole-burnt peace-offering of thanksgiving to the Lord, and should open for himself the gate looking eastward" (Ezek. 46:12, VP), as well as, "And the glory of the Lord came into the house, by the way of the gate looking eastward" (Ezek. 43:4, VP). In the New Testament also, significance is attached to the east, particularly in regard to both the first and second comings of Christ:

Where is He who has been born King of the Jews? For we have seen His star in the East and have come to worship Him. (Matt. 2:2, NKJV)

For as the lightning comes from the east and flashes to the west, so also will the coming of the Son of Man be. (Matt. 24:27, NKJV)

The priest asks, "Do you join Christ?" three times, and the candidate replies, "I do join Him." Having rejected the devil, the candidate is now free to declare his faith in Christ, and he then recites the Creed. In cases of infant baptism, the responses and the Creed are recited by the godparent on the child's behalf.

The second half of the baptism service begins as does the Divine Liturgy, with an opening blessing: "Blessed is the Kingdom of the Father, and of the Son and of the Holy Spirit." Most Orthodox services begin with "Blessed is our God, always, now and forever." The reason that baptism begins as does the Liturgy is because the service of baptism used to be held during the Divine Liturgy, particularly the Easter Liturgy. Thus baptism, like the Liturgy, is a journey to the Kingdom of Heaven. That journey, of course, for each of us, begins at our baptism. Whether the candidate for baptism is a child or an adult, whether he has converted to the Faith or is of an age where he cannot understand the Faith, a new life is about to begin.

▶ The reason the priest during most of the Divine Liturgy and other services has his back to the people is because all the people face eastward with the priest. The services and Sacraments of the Church are not ceremonies the priest performs for the people to watch like spectators at a theater. The people are praying and offering with the priest.

▶ Why do we baptize infants, given they cannot understand their faith or choose baptism for themselves? The answer is quite straightforward: infants are more suitable for baptism than anyone. As Christ said, "Let the little children come to me and do not hinder them, for to such belongs the kingdom of heaven" (Matt. 19:14, ESV). Children, being pure and innocent, and being fit for the Kingdom of Heaven, are the most receptive to the Holy Spirit. Also, the Church is a family. We do not exclude our children from our families, so we do not exclude them from the spiritual family that is our Church. We do not prohibit our children from eating with us at the dinner table, so we do not prohibit them from partaking of Holy Communion at Christ's altar.

The priest then leads the congregation in prayer for the descent of the Holy Spirit upon the baptismal water and for the salvation of the one to be baptized.

Water is essential to and a symbol of life, for nothing can survive without it. It is also the symbol of purification, since water is necessary for cleanliness. And water also is a symbol of death, since it can also be destructive, as we have seen in the Old Testament stories of Noah and the Flood (Gen. 7) and the drowning of the Egyptians in the Red Sea (Exod. 14), and in our own day in tsunamis, hurricanes, and floods. And so, when we immerse a child—or an adult—into those blessed waters, the act is wrought with meaning. Above all, the immersion of the baptized in the water represents the death of "the old man" (that is, the person of the flesh), the washing away of sin, and the new life of the risen Christ.

The blessing of the water is followed by the anointing with oil of the candidate for baptism. Oil is also a material object that is imbued with deep spiritual meanings. Oil is a symbol of the Holy Spirit, of Christ (the "Anointed One"), and of Kingship. But in ancient times it was also used for healing. The Good Samaritan (Lk. 10:25–37) pours wine and oil into the wounds of the robbed victim. Oil was also, of course, a means of light and was once essential for illumination in any kind of darkness—at home, in church, at nighttime. The oil is therefore a symbol of light, healing, and joy.

Then comes the big moment that friends and family, and other members of the Church, have been waiting for—what gives all the prayers and preparation full meaning. The priest immerses the candidate in the water three times, saying "The servant of God . . . is baptised in the name of the Father, and of the Son, and of the Holy Spirit." We say it precisely this way in obedience to our Lord's injunction two thousand years ago: "Make disciples of all nations, baptizing them in the name of the Father and of the Son and of the Holy Spirit" (Matt. 28:19, ESV). We call this the threefold immersion, and sometimes a "burial," in the water to signify that the baptized one is participating in Christ's death, burial, and resurrection on the third day. The meaning of this is summed up by St. Paul in his Epistle to the Romans, which is the appointed Epistle Reading for baptism (6:3–11):

> Brethren, as many of us as were baptised into Christ were baptised into his death. We were buried then with him through baptism to death, so that, just as Christ was raised from the dead through the glory of the Father, we too might walk in newness of life. For if we have grown into union with him through a death like his, we shall also be united with him in the resurrection. For we know that our old self was crucified with him, so that our sinful body might be done away with, that we might no longer be in slavery to sin. For one who has died has been justified from sin. If then we died with Christ, we believe

that we shall also live with him. For we know
that Christ, being raised from the dead, dies
no more; death no longer lords it over him. As
to dying, he died once and for all; as to living,
he lives for God. Consequently, you also must
consider yourselves dead to sin, but alive to God
in Christ Jesus our Lord. (EL)

Immediately after the baptism in the water, the
newly baptized one is anointed with the chrism—holy
myrrh—which we know was one of the gifts brought
to the Christ child from the wise men of the east. The
priest anoints the head, face, body, and limbs of the
newly illumined, each time saying, "The seal of the
gift of the Holy Spirit." The gift of the Holy Spirit is
union with God and a new life in the risen Christ.
Chrismation is our own personal Pentecost. Just as the
Holy Spirit descended upon the Apostles in Jerusalem
(Acts 1), so He descends also upon us when we are
anointed in baptism.

The baptized one is then dressed in a white garment,
which is the liturgical color of the Resurrection and
of purity. The "newly illumined" is therefore clothed
with Christ, with the life of the Resurrection and of
the world to come. He is led in procession around the
baptismal font as the priest censes around the font,
singing a verse from St. Paul's Epistle to the Romans:
"As many as have been baptised into Christ, have put

on Christ. Alleluia!" That is the significance of the white garment. In baptism we are made sharers of Christ's life, of His divine life, of His Resurrection. We are made one with Him, members of His Body. Our body has been endowed with a divine quality and potential. Just as Christ's body was transfigured on Mount Tabor, and shone even brighter than the sun (Matt. 17:1–9), just as it was transfigured and renewed in His Resurrection, so too our bodies are destined for transfiguration and renewal.

Toward the end of the baptism ceremony (or after the Chrismation), we have the tonsure—the cutting of the hair. This is the first offering of the baptized to God—a piece of oneself—a perfect offering. Tonsure also takes place at the making of monks and "minor clerics," such as Readers and Chanters. It is therefore the symbol of dedication to Christ and His Church.

These three actions—baptism, Chrismation, tonsure—mark our consecration and complete dedication to God.

▶ Because catechumens were once baptized during the Divine Liturgy on great feasts such as Easter, Christmas, and Theophany, the Trisagion Hymn at the Liturgy on those feast days is replaced by the hymn, "As many as have been baptised into Christ, have put on Christ. Alleluia!"

It is quite common for the newly baptized to receive their first Communion immediately after baptism or at the earliest opportunity. St. John Chrysostom compares baptism to childbirth, and the baptismal font to the womb. Just as a baby, as soon as it is born, goes straight to its mother's breast to be nurtured, so too when a person is "reborn" in the baptismal font, he is immediately brought to the Holy Chalice to be spiritually nurtured. Holy Communion then becomes the seal and "fulfillment" of baptism. Even the infant has become a full member of the Church who should be brought to receive Communion frequently from the time of baptism.

Holy Communion is the confirmation of our membership in the Church. We are truly members of the Orthodox Church in the fullest sense as long as we continually renew our baptism in Holy Communion. Thus baptism and the Divine Liturgy are intimately connected. It is through baptism that we are given access to the Kingdom of God, to the heavenly banquet that is the Divine Liturgy. At every Liturgy, we are extended the invitation to partake of this banquet, in which we have a foretaste of the Kingdom of Heaven. As the Lord said to the Apostles: "I bestow upon you a kingdom, just as My Father bestowed *one* upon Me, that you may eat and drink at My table in My kingdom" (Lk. 22:29–30, NKJV).

15. *Dome with icons of Christ, angels, and saints*

❖ 15 ❖

The Creed: Resurrection

*You brought us out of non-existence into being,
and when we had fallen you raised us up again,
and left nothing undone until you had brought
us up to heaven and had granted us your
Kingdom that is to come.*

—Prayer of the Holy Oblation,
Liturgy of St. John Chrysostom

"If Christ has not risen, then our preaching is in vain, and your faith also is in vain" (1 Cor. 15:14, vp). So wrote St. Paul to the Christians of Corinth in the middle of the first century. Orthodox Christianity hangs on the Resurrection. This is where, as the saying goes, the rubber meets the road. If Christ, the Son of God, did not die and rise from the dead that we may have eternal life, then there is no salvation for humanity. Thus we proclaim at the end of the Creed, "I await the resurrection of the dead and the life of the age to come."

Christ's Resurrection is therefore of vital importance to our belief in the Resurrection of all humanity. For this reason, some Christians go to a lot of effort to "prove" that the Resurrection really happened. They try to persuade unbelievers by appealing to the "historical" details in Scripture. But it seems to me that the Gospel writers deliberately avoided this approach (as I will demonstrate below). You simply cannot prove that Jesus rose from the dead in the same way that you can prove He suffered and died under Pontius Pilate. In fact, *believing* that Jesus Christ is not just a man, but the Son of God Who rose from the dead, is so essential to being a Christian that trying to turn it into a simple matter of fact undermines the life-changing power of its significance. At the end of St. John's Gospel, we read, "These things are written that you may believe . . ." (John 20:31, vp), not, "These things are written to prove. . . ."

The Resurrection is so vital to Orthodoxy that it is the most important and splendid celebration of the church year. The Orthodox Church is, in fact, often described as the Church of the Resurrection, as it is so central to what we do and believe.

The promise of Resurrection is at the heart of our celebration. Christ's Resurrection is not completely disconnected from our own. Our Lord did not rise from the dead for Himself, but for us. God became flesh and blood in order to redeem our fallen nature, to deliver us from eternal death and to give us new, everlasting life. The Church therefore believes in what is commonly called "the General Resurrection," that is, the Resurrection of all human beings.

Almost all religions believe in an afterlife, that the soul lives on after death. But Christianity proclaims something more than this. We believe in the Resurrection of the body. The human body and the material world are not things from which we are to escape and which are to be shunned and despised. The material world will be transfigured, just as Christ's body was on Mount Tabor (Lk. 9:28–36), just as it was at the Resurrection (Lk. 24:13–16, 30–31, 36–38; 1 Cor. 15:42–54). Christ manifested to us the reality of His bodily Resurrection when He appeared to the apostles and they felt His hands and side and when He ate with them.

And Christ's Resurrection was not merely the resuscitation of a corpse. Christ was not a mere ghost after the Resurrection: He ate with the disciples, and Thomas even felt His hands and side. Yet in the same Gospel records, whenever Christ appears to His followers and apostles after His Resurrection, no one recognizes Him, until He does or says something that makes them realize that it is Jesus, and His risen body evidently was not bound by the laws of nature.

The accounts of our Lord's Resurrection in the Gospels make up the eleven Sunday Matins Gospel Readings (*Eothina Evangelia*). These Readings of the accounts of our Lord's Resurrection (and they are read on Sundays because Sunday is the day of the Resurrection) are proclaimed during the Matins Service (*Orthros*) from the altar, which represents Christ's tomb, and they signify and forever renew the angelic proclamation, "Christ has risen! Spread the good news!"

The fifth Sunday Matins Gospel (Lk. 24:12–35) tells us of the first Easter Sunday, when two of Christ's disciples are walking to Emmaus, discussing the tragedy of Christ's death. Christ Himself joins them, but they do not recognize Him, and they think He is a mere visitor to the area. They do not recognize Him even after He joins in the conversation and explains to them that the death of Christ was foretold in the Scriptures. Inspired by His explanation of the Scriptures, they urge Him to stay with them in Emmaus and invite Him to eat with them, and only after He blesses and breaks the bread and gives it to them and then vanishes from their sight do they recognize Him as Christ.

In the eighth Gospel Reading (John 20:11–18), Mary Magdalene also sees the risen Christ, but we are told that she thought He was the gardener. Only when He speaks her name does she realize it is Jesus.

Again, in the third Gospel Reading (Mark 16:9–20), we are told the risen Christ appeared to Mary Magdalene, and He tells her to let the Apostles know that He has risen, and they do not believe her. We then read that Christ Himself appeared to two of them "in another form," and when they tell the others, they still do not believe.

In the tenth Gospel Reading (John 21:1–14), the Apostles go fishing, and the risen Christ appears on the shore, and they do not recognize Him. He asks if they have something to eat, and they say no. He tells them to cast their net to the right and they will find something, and when they do so the net is suddenly filled to bursting. Only after this miraculous catch of fish (a miracle Christ wrought during His earthly life, which no doubt the Apostles immediately recalled) does John recognize Christ, and says to Peter, "It is the Lord." They then eat with Him, and we are told that "none of them dared ask, 'Who are you?' knowing that it was the Lord (VP)".

Clearly there is a great mystery here. There was nothing about the body of the risen Christ by which those who knew Him could physically recognize Him. Some may think that the story in the ninth Matins Gospel (John 20:19–31) contradicts this. In this reading, we hear of the unbelief of Thomas, when he states, "Unless I see in His hands the print of the nails, and put my finger into the print of the nails, and put my hand into His side, I will not believe" (NKJV). Christ then appears and shows Thomas the wounds of which he spoke and offers him the opportunity to do as he said. But it was not "proof" but belief that Christ offered him. Judging by the other Gospel narratives, there may have been nothing by which Thomas could have recognized the Lord but the wounds, and Christ asks him to "be not an unbeliever but a believer" (VP). Before Thomas even takes up the offer, he believes and proclaims, "My Lord and my God!" (NKJV).

Now, add to this mystery the curious fact that there is no description of the Resurrection itself in the Gospels. We are told that Christ is buried, and then the next day when the women go to anoint the body, they find the stone of the tomb rolled away and the body not there, and yet the shroud has been left behind. The body of Christ had no need for the shroud. For it was no longer a body like ours. Note the difference between the *anastasis* ("Resurrection") of Christ and the *ergesis* ("Raising") of Lazarus (John 11:1–45). In the Gospel account, when Christ restores Lazarus to life he comes out of the tomb in the burial shroud. He was no different from how he was before he died. Christ's body after His Resurrection, however, seems very different indeed. He is there one moment and gone the next. He takes on different forms. Finally, He ascends into the heavens to return to His Father. All of this tells us that the body of the risen Christ, and therefore our own bodies at the final Resurrection, will not be the same kind of body we now possess. The very nature of our bodies will be transformed and transfigured. The body of Christ in His earthly life was, like ours, subject to pain, fatigue, hunger, thirst, and so on. But following the Resurrection, this is not the case. When we speak of the Resurrection, we are speaking of a new life, a new creation. This is why Christ says, "Behold, I am making all things new" (Rev. 21:5, ESV).

But does all of this really matter? Many people today think the Church is failing in its duty to make this world a better place by being so focused on the "world to come." They think that concerning ourselves with heaven and hell, with life after death and Resurrection, is a waste of time. Why not just focus on improving *this* world? The answer is simple: how we fare in the next life depends on how we live this one. The more we care about eternity, the more we will care about the here and now. In the words of C. S. Lewis:

> If you read history you will find that the Christians who did most for the present world were just those who thought most of the next. The Apostles themselves, who set on foot the conversion of the Roman Empire, the great men who built up the Middle Ages, the English Evangelicals who abolished the Slave Trade, all left their mark on Earth, precisely because their minds were occupied with Heaven. It is since Christians have largely ceased to think of the other world that they have become so ineffective in this. Aim at Heaven and you will get earth "thrown in": aim at earth and you will get neither.[27]

16. *Icon of the Pelican as a metaphor for Christ in the Eucharist [Greek inscription:* **"Like the pelican, you gave life, O Word, to your dead children; wounded in your side, you let life-blood flow, letting fall life-giving drops of blood on all."** *(Second Stanza from the Lamentations of the Matins Service for Great and Holy Saturday)]*

❖ 16 ❖

The Holy Oblation

In Cana of Galilee, Christ turned water into wine,
and shall we think Him less worthy of credit when
He turns wine into His Blood?
—St. Cyril of Jerusalem

During the chanting of the Creed—which takes much less "real" time than it took you to read those chapters!—the priest has been removing the veil from the Holy Gifts. This indicates a shift to yet another gear in the Liturgy.

We are now to begin the most solemn part of the Liturgy, known as the *Agia Anaphora*, the Holy Oblation, at the heart of which is the commemoration of Christ's Last Supper and the transformation of the bread and wine into the Lord's Body and Blood.

We hear the exclamation:

Let us stand with awe; let us stand with fear;
let us attend to the holy oblation that in peace
we may offer: mercy, peace: a sacrifice of praise.

Mercy and peace: that is the sacrifice God asks of us. But to offer this, we must acknowledge first that we have fallen short of God's mercy and peace. We must turn to God in repentance, put aside all hatred and animosity, all pride and injustice, and be reconciled with one another. For we cannot offer mercy and peace if we have none. The Prophet Isaiah puts it very strongly:

> What do I care for the number of your sacrifices? says the Lord. I have had enough of whole-burnt rams and fat of fatlings. I take no pleasure in the blood of calves, lambs and goats. When you come in to visit me, who asks these things of you? Trample my courts no more! Bring no more worthless offerings; your incense is loathsome to me. . . . I detest your new moons and festivals; they weigh me down, I am tired of the load. When you spread out your hands, I close my eyes to you. Though you pray even more, I will not listen. Your hands are full of blood! Wash yourselves clean! Put away your misdeeds from before my eyes; stop doing evil; learn to do good. Make justice your aim: redress the wronged, hear the orphan's plea, defend the widow. (Isa. 1:11–17, EL)

The priest then blesses the people with an ancient blessing found in the Epistles of St. Paul:

The grace of our Lord Jesus Christ, and the love of God the Father, and the communion of the Holy Spirit be with you all.

"Let our hearts be on high," says the priest; and the people respond, "We have them with the Lord." Our Liturgy has taken us into the heights of heaven. During the Liturgy we become like the angels; we have a foretaste of the life of God's Kingdom, which eternally resounds with the praise of God. "Let us give thanks to the Lord," the priest exclaims, and he says a prayer of thanksgiving for all that Christ has done for us.

In the Liturgy of St. Basil the Great, this prayer is considerably longer than in the Liturgy of St. John Chrysostom, which is usually celebrated. But at the end of the prayer in both liturgies, the priest goes on to refer to the thousands of angels and archangels, the Cherubim and the Seraphim, who are ever singing the hymn that the choir now sings at the Liturgy: "Holy, holy, holy, Lord Sabaoth; heaven and earth are full of your glory." I have spoken of this thrice-holy hymn of the angels before. We sang it after the Entrance of the Gospel: "Holy God, Holy Strong, Holy Immortal. . . ." We were reminded of it again before the Great Entrance: "We who represent the Cherubim and sing the thrice-holy hymn to the life-giving Trinity." Now we sing it again in imitation of the angels in heaven: "Holy, holy, holy, Lord Sabaoth. . . ." Our Liturgy on earth is joined with the eternal liturgy in heaven. Our hearts should be on high, devoted to the adoration of the Trinity and immersed in the holy presence of God.

After the thrice-holy hymn, the priest recalls the Mystical Supper, when Christ offered bread and wine to His Apostles before His betrayal, suffering, and crucifixion, and ordered them to do this in memory of Him: "Take, eat; this is my body, which is broken for you, for the forgiveness of sins." "Drink of this, all of you; this is my blood of the New Covenant, which is shed for you and for many for the forgiveness of sins." And remembering all that Christ has done for us, the priest elevates the gifts and exclaims: "Offering you your own from your own, in all things and for all things—we praise you, we bless you, we give thanks to you, O Lord, and we pray to you our God." We have nothing to offer God but what is already His own. The human being is the priest of creation. His vocation is to offer creation back to the Creator in praise and thanksgiving. The prime example of this is the Eucharist. The bread and wine we offer belong to Him. It is ours only by His benevolent grace and providence. And so at the Liturgy we offer it back that He may make it His Body and Blood for the forgiveness of sins and eternal life.

The offering is followed by what is called the *epiclesis*, a Greek word that literally means "to call down"—that is the point at the Liturgy when the clergy call on the Holy Spirit to change this bread and wine into the Body and

Blood of Christ. In the Liturgy of St. John Chrysostom, while the choir is chanting, the priest prays:

> We ask, pray and implore you: send down your Holy Spirit upon us and upon these gifts here set forth, and make this bread the precious Body of your Christ, and what is in this Cup the precious Blood of your Christ, changing them by your Holy Spirit, so that those who partake of them may obtain vigilance of soul, forgiveness of sins, communion of your Holy Spirit, fullness of the Kingdom of heaven, freedom to speak in your presence, not judgement or condemnation.

Now Christ is physically present with us. The Lord comes to us time and again in the form of bread and wine, that He may be one with us. The bread and wine of course look, taste, and feel no different from ordinary

▶ The Orthodox use leavened bread for the Eucharist. While the Synoptic Gospels (Matthew, Mark, and Luke) present the Last Supper as a Passover meal—when the Jews used only unleavened bread—John's Gospel emphasizes that it took place before the Passover. In this matter, the Orthodox Church has always followed John's Gospel.

bread and wine, but they are also the Lord's Body and Blood. Just as Christ is both divine and human, so is the Eucharist both body and yet bread, blood and yet wine. The Lord offers us His flesh in this way that we may be able to receive Him.

"I am the bread of life" (John 6:35), says the Lord. "Whoever eats my flesh and drinks my blood has eternal life. . . . For my flesh is real food and my blood is real drink" (John 6:54–55, NIV). God offers us His flesh and blood in love.

This love of Christ in the Eucharist is expressed in a beautiful but rare icon of Christ portrayed as a pelican. In Christian history, the mother pelican was thought to pierce her breast until she bled in order to feed her young with her blood. Thus the pelican came to depict Christ our Savior, who feeds us with His blood in order to give us eternal life. In this image, the pelican is a metaphor for Christ in the Eucharist. The Eucharist reminds us of Christ's sacrifice, of the pain and suffering He chose to endure in His love for us. It is for this reason that some of our saints were known to have been in tears at every Eucharist. They cried every time they came to receive Communion because in the Eucharist they saw how much God loved them.

May we too begin to see Christ's love for us at every Divine Liturgy!

◈ 17 ◈

Remembrance

Whenever you eat this bread and drink this cup,
you proclaim the Lord's death until he comes.
—1 COR. 11:26, NIV

Remembrance is the basis of so many celebrations, religious and secular. People of all creeds and of none celebrate the memory of those who died, the beginning of a new year, their wedding anniversaries, their birthdays. So too in the Divine Liturgy, remembrance is very important. The Liturgy is celebrated in obedience to Christ's command: "Do this in remembrance of me" (Lk. 22:19, NIV).

In the Divine Liturgy, remembrance is not just a matter of calling to mind, of remembering things or people of the past. It has a more profound meaning than that. It means to bring to the forefront of our thoughts, of our prayer, to bring before God, to make present at the Holy Altar the past and, indeed, the future. In this connection, it is worth noting that after the consecration of the bread and wine, the clergy

17. *Bishop elevating the Holy Gifts*

(*"Offering you your own from your own ..."*)

remember, on behalf of the congregation, the Second Coming—something that is yet to come:

> Remembering therefore this our Saviour's command and all that has been done for us: the Cross, the Tomb, the Resurrection on the third day, the Ascension into heaven, the Sitting at the right hand, the Second and glorious Coming again. . . .

The Liturgy is "timeless" (and it can sometimes feel like that!) because God is beyond time and space, and so at the Divine Liturgy, all things—past, present, future—are brought together before God's altar. Therefore, after the consecration of the bread and wine, we remember all the living and all the departed. The living and the departed form one Church, one spiritual family. Divine love is not conscious of visible separation. The priest says:

> Also we offer you this spiritual worship for those who have gone to their rest in faith, Forefathers, Fathers, Patriarchs, Prophets, Apostles, Preachers, Evangelists, Martyrs, Confessors, Ascetics and every righteous spirit made perfect in faith; Above all for our most holy, pure, most blessed and glorious Lady, Mother of God and Ever-virgin, Mary.

The choir then sings a hymn to the Mother of God. While this hymn is being sung, the priest censes the gifts on the altar and continues to pray—for John the Baptist, the Apostles, the saints of the day, and all the saints—and then he says:

Remember too all those who have fallen asleep in hope of resurrection to eternal life, and give them rest where the light of your countenance watches.

Because the clergy say these prayers quietly during this hymn to the Mother of God, most people have no idea that we pray for the departed at this very solemn moment of the Liturgy. The Church is made up not only of those who are physically present at the Liturgy but also those who have passed on. We remember them and pray for them as members of the Church.

The Prayer of Remembrance goes on and, in St. Basil's Liturgy, is greatly extended, as we pray for the clergy, the people, the local authorities, for the married, for children and young people and families, as well as for monks and nuns, for the sick, and for the poor:

Remember, Lord, the people here present and those who are absent for good reason, and have mercy on them and on us according to the multitude of your mercy . . . preserve their marriages in peace and concord; nourish the infants, guide the young, strengthen the aged; comfort the fainthearted; gather the scattered; bring back those who have gone astray, and join them to your holy, catholic and apostolic Church. Free those who are troubled by unclean spirits; sail with those who sail; journey with those who journey; champion widows; protect orphans; deliver prisoners; heal the sick.

"We are thus reminded," writes Fr. Ephrem Lash, "that the Liturgy is not just about ourselves . . . that there are two great commandments, to love God and to love our fellow human beings. St. John Chrysostom often ends his sermons by reminding his congregation that if they want to find Christ they will find him in the beggars that sit asking for alms outside the doors of the church."[28]

Take for example this beautiful passage:

If you want to honor Christ, do it when you see him naked in the person of the poor. Do not honor him here in the church with silken garments and precious metals while neglecting him outside where he is cold and naked. . . . God does not want vessels of gold, but hearts of gold. In saying this I am not forbidding you to offer such gifts; I am only saying that along with such gifts and before them you should give alms. He accepts the former, but he is much more pleased with the latter.[29]

After the hymn to the Mother of God, the petitions of remembrance continue:

First of all, remember, Lord, our Archbishop . . . and grant that he may serve your holy churches in peace, safety, honour, health and length of days, rightly discerning the word of your truth.

And those whom each one has in mind, and each and all.

We then begin the Litany of the Lord's Prayer. So great is the importance attached to this prayer that we pray before we say it!

Having commemorated all the saints, again and again in peace, let us pray to the Lord.

For the precious gifts here set forth and sanctified, let us pray to the Lord.

That our God, who loves mankind, having accepted them on his holy and immaterial altar above the heavens, as a savour of spiritual fragrance, may send down upon us in return his divine grace and the gift of the Holy Spirit, let us pray.

While the deacon says this, the priest prays:

Count us worthy to partake of your heavenly and awesome Mysteries at this sacred and spiritual Table with a pure conscience, for forgiveness of sins and pardon of offences, for communion of the Holy Spirit, for inheritance of the Kingdom of Heaven and for confidence before you; not for judgement or condemnation.

The priest then exclaims:

And count us worthy, Master, with confidence and without condemnation to dare to call upon you, the God of heaven, as Father, and to say . . .

We then all say the Lord's Prayer, the only prayer that our Lord gave us, which is said at every service of the Church and at every Divine Liturgy just before we receive Holy Communion. And that will be the subject of the following chapter.

18. *Bishop blessing the people*

• 18 •

The Lord's Prayer

If we are his children, then we are heirs—
heirs of God and fellow heirs with Christ.
—Rom. 8:17, vp

The Lord's Prayer, or the "Our Father," is undoubtedly the most important and best-known prayer in Christianity. This is hardly surprising, since it is the one and only prayer that Christ Himself gave us:

> Our Father in heaven, may your name be sanctified, your kingdom come, your will be done on earth as in heaven. Give us today our daily bread, and forgive us our debts, as we forgive our debtors; and do not lead us into temptation, but deliver us from the evil one.

Our Father

We address God as Father. God is a personal God. He is not the god of philosophers, merely to be talked about and contemplated, but the God of Abraham, Isaac, and Jacob—a God who intervenes in human history, Who loves us and cares for us. Thus God is our Father, and we are His children.

A comedian once quipped: "If we are all God's children, then what's so special about Jesus?" But obviously he missed the point. We are God's children by divine adoption. In becoming a human being like us, Christ has made us His brothers and sisters. That is why the priest introduces the Our Father by saying, "And count us worthy, Master, with confidence . . . to dare to call upon you, the God of heaven, as Father." In St. John's Gospel we read: "To all who did receive him, to those who believed in his name, he gave the right to become children of God" (John 1:12, NIV). To Mary Magdalene, the risen Lord says: "Go . . . to my brothers and tell them, 'I am ascending to my Father and your Father, to my God and your God'" (John 20:17, NIV).

May Your Name Be Sanctified

The name of God is sanctified—that is, holy, hallowed, blessed. We bless the name of God, not because God needs our blessing, but because this is the priestly way of life, the life of all Christians—to bless and offer back to God all that already belongs to Him. Therefore, we bless His holy name.

Your Kingdom Come, Your Will Be Done on Earth as in Heaven

This world is not the Kingdom of God. We live in a fallen world, a world that is far from perfect, far from what God wants it to be. From the earliest times, Christians have longed and prayed for this Kingdom of God that is to come. This Kingdom exists already in heaven. In the Church, it has already arrived on earth, but at the same time it is yet to come, yet to be fulfilled and perfected. Many Christians believe that this world will come to an end and that we will all be in Heaven at the end of all things. But the truth is that Christianity does not believe in the end of the world, but in the renewal or transfiguration of the world. In the last book of the Bible, the book of Revelation, St. John sees a vision of the Kingdom of Heaven coming to earth:

> Then I saw a new heaven and a new earth, for the first heaven and the first earth had passed away, and the sea was no more. And I saw the holy city, new Jerusalem, coming down out of heaven from God, prepared as a bride adorned for her husband. And I heard a loud

voice from the throne saying, "Behold, the dwelling place of God is with man. He will dwell with them, and they will be his people, and God himself will be with them as their God. He will wipe away every tear from their eyes, and death shall be no more, neither shall there be mourning, nor crying, nor pain anymore, for the former things have passed away." And he who was seated on the throne said, "Behold, I am making all things new." (Rev. 21:1–5, ESV)

Give Us Today Our Daily Bread

We ask only for what is necessary for the day. As our Lord said:

> I tell you, do not worry about your life, what you will eat or drink; or about your body, what you will wear. Is not life more than food, and the body more than clothes? Look at the birds of the air; they do not sow or reap or store away in barns, and yet your heavenly Father feeds them. Are you not much more valuable than they? Can any one of you by worrying add a single hour to your life? And why do you worry about clothes? See how the flowers of the field grow. They do not labor or spin. Yet I tell you that not even Solomon in all his splendor was dressed like

one of these. If that is how God clothes the grass of the field, which is here today and tomorrow is thrown into the fire, will he not much more clothe you—you of little faith? So do not worry, saying, "What shall we eat?" or "What shall we drink?" or "What shall we wear?" For the pagans run after all these things, and your heavenly Father knows that you need them. But seek first his kingdom and his righteousness, and all these things will be given to you as well. (Matt. 6:25–33, NIV)

The Greek word for "daily" in this prayer (*epiousion*) is most unusual. In fact, some argue that "daily" is actually a poor translation for this word. They say that *epiousios* comes from *ousia* ("essence") and *epi* ("upon or above"), and therefore *arton* ("bread") *epiousion* does not refer to ordinary food, not to "daily bread," but rather to that bread which is over and above the essential. It is in this way that St. Maximus the Confessor says that *arton epiousion* is the bread of life, that is, Holy Communion. This is the reason that the Our Father is recited just before Holy Communion. However, St. John Chrysostom also states quite plainly that *epiousios* means simply *ephemeron* ("of the day").

Forgive Us Our Debts as
We Forgive Our Debtors

It is probably above all because of the phrase "forgive us our debts as we forgive our debtors" that the Our Father was placed here, just before the Communion of the clergy and the people, in our Divine Liturgy. In the Gospel our Lord says: "If you are offering your gift at the altar and there remember that your brother has something against you, leave your gift there before the altar and go. First be reconciled to your brother, and then come and offer your gift" (Matt. 5:23–24, ESV).

So too before Communion, we must forgive everyone from the bottom of our heart and be reconciled with one another. Without this forgiveness, our Liturgy is not pleasing to God. The Lord puts it very plainly in the Gospel: "If you forgive others their offences, God will also forgive your offences; but if you do not forgive others, neither will God forgive you" (Matt. 6:14–15, VP).

We should not see Communion as a mechanical or magical thing—as though we receive forgiveness of sins just by the process of eating and drinking the Lord's Body and Blood. The whole point of the Liturgy is not just to sing songs but to prepare us for the Sacrament of Communion, to soften our hearts that we may receive the grace and mercy of God, "that we may pursue a spiritual way of life, thinking and doing all things that are pleasing to you," as we say in the prayer before the reading of the Gospel.

And Do Not Lead Us into Temptation, but Deliver Us from the Evil One

We pray that God will not abandon us to temptations too great for us to bear. Anyone who is familiar with biblical language will notice that the word "temptation" is often used in connection with suffering or persecution. Temptation does not just mean being enticed by pleasures, like food or sex. Temptation often takes the form of violence and persecution. In this context, temptation is above all the temptation to lose faith, hope, patience, courage, and love of God. The book of Revelation frequently mentions temptation in this context, and it appeals to the patience of the Christians to endure it, reminding them of their great reward in heaven. But in the context of being enticed into sin, such as sex or gluttony (which nowadays, alas, seem to be the only contexts in which the word "temptation" is used) temptation is not the same thing as sin.

Temptation is something we will experience throughout our life until our last breath. We know that the devil tempts us, but too many Christians use the devil as a scapegoat, a way of shifting responsibility for our sins to something outside of ourselves and beyond our control. It is not a sin to be tempted. The greatest of saints experienced great temptation. But acting upon the temptation, giving into it, is where sin begins. In fact, the righteous experience temptation more than anybody, and the temptations for them are perhaps far more powerful and violent than they are for many of us, for the devil is eager to destroy the souls of the righteous. I cannot imagine that the devil bothers so much with those who reject God and choose sin as a way of life. Wherever Christ is, we should expect the devil to be also.

Even Christ Himself was tempted by the devil (Mark 1:12–13; see also Matt. 16:23). That is why we should not be surprised to find sin and evil within the Church. But we should not think that every animal instinct, every desire, is a sin in itself. We have a fallen nature. We often feel our instincts conflicting with our conscience, with what we know is good and proper. It is not that those instincts are bad in themselves, but there is a time and a place and a proper proportion for everything. We need God's help to control and master the passions. The devil tempts us but does not choose for us. Neither does God choose for us. He calls and invites us to love and follow Him, and He warns us against sin, but He does not compel us. For we cannot love God at all unless we have freely chosen to do so.

❖ 19 ❖

Holy Things for the Holy

Be holy, for I am holy.
—Lev. 11:44, esv

At this point there is often an air of anticipation in the Liturgy. Just about every Orthodox churchgoer knows that the "Our Father" ushers in the time for Holy Communion. But there is still more praying to be done.

The priest blesses the people again, and we are told to bow our heads to the Lord, and the priest prays for the "need of each: sail with those who sail, journey with those who journey, heal the sick, for you are the physician of our souls and bodies."

This prayer just before Communion may seem out of place. It seems to have no relationship to Communion itself. Instead it addresses our needs after Communion or the needs of those who are not with us. But if you think about it, there is nothing all that strange about

19. *Bishop receiving Holy Communion*

it being placed here. We call receiving the Body and Blood of Christ Communion because it unites us not only with Christ but also with one another. Therefore the needs of our fellow human beings should be felt as though they are our own.

The clergy then pray:

> Give heed, Lord Jesus Christ our God, from your holy dwelling-place and from the glorious throne of your kingdom; and come to sanctify us, you who are enthroned on high with the Father and invisibly present here with us. And with your mighty hand grant communion in your most pure Body and precious Blood to us, and through us to all the people.

The deacon then exclaims, "Let us attend!" and the priest, elevating the bread that is now the Body of Christ, exclaims, "The Holy things for the holy [ones]." We are the holy ones, not by any virtue of our own, but because we are members of Christ's Body. The full implication of this intimate union between Christ and His people is conveyed in one of the most beautiful biblical images of the Church: that of the Bride of Christ. By making Himself one with us, He has sanctified us. Through this mystical union with our Lord, we are made sharers of His holiness. Again let us return to the words of St. Paul: "Christ loved the Church and gave himself for her, that he might sanctify her, having purified her with the washing of water with a word, that he might present the Church to himself glorious, without spot or wrinkle or anything similar, but that she might be holy and unblemished" (Eph. 5:25–27, EL).

Since we are holy only because Christ is holy, the choir then sings: "One is holy, one is Lord: Jesus Christ, to the glory of God the Father, Amen."

We are all called to be "holy ones," or "saints" (*hagioi*). Holiness, or sainthood, is not the calling of a select few, but of every Christian. But the saints are not perfect beings. We do not become saints by never making a mistake, by never falling into sin; we become saints through continuous repentance.

Many of the saints lived very sinful lives until conversion. Some were guilty of murder, adultery, prostitution, idol-worship, and all manner of terrible sins. But we should not think that the saints were perfect after conversion either. Someone once asked, "What do monks do in monasteries all day?" The reply: "We fall and get up, fall and get up again." That is repentance. That is how we become saints. This has been beautifully expressed by the American author Phyllis McGinley: "The wonderful thing about saints is that they were *human*. They lost their tempers, got hungry, scolded God, were egotistical or testy or impatient in their turns, made mistakes and regretted them. Still they went on doggedly blundering toward heaven."[30]

Still, the saints, while attaining the likeness of God, never ceased to be who they were. The greatest misconception about sanctity or sainthood is that to be a saint we must give up our own personalities. People tend to think that to be a saint one must become a sheepish, humorless person, with no idiosyncrasies or personal tastes or interests. But anyone who cares to spend time reading about the lives of saints will notice that while they may have much in common, they are also very different. As C. S. Lewis aptly wrote: "How monotonously alike all the great tyrants and conquerors have been: how gloriously different are the saints."[31] Similarly, Metropolitan Kallistos of Diokelia writes: "The saints, so far from displaying a drab monotony, have developed the most vivid and distinctive personalities. It is not holiness, but evil which is dull."[32]

While each of us has our own unique personality and charisma, the true personhood of each person is distorted by sin. We are not to accept ourselves blindly as we are, with all our faults and shortcomings, warts and all. Rather, we are to *become* what we truly *are*. What does this mean? It means that my true self can only be discovered by cutting away the sin, which distorts my true personality. The saints are therefore those who possess the fullness of personhood, who have the truest, purest personalities. The holier we become, the more sin is cut away, the more of our true selves we discover.

Returning now to the Liturgy: while the choir sings, the clergy receive Communion in the Sanctuary and then prepare the Communion to give to the people, placing the bread into the Chalice with the wine. Communion is given to the people in a spoon, with a portion of the bread and wine together. Unfortunately, in many of our churches, we seem to have a sort of interval at this point—money collections, a sermon, announcements, whatnot. But this is really not the right place for such things. There should not be such a great gap between the Communion of the clergy and the Communion of the people. We are all equally called to receive Communion. It is not the privilege of the clergy. During the Communion of the clergy, the people can be preparing themselves for Holy Communion, which means we quietly pray, forgiving those who have wronged us, confessing our sins to God.

Once the Chalice is prepared, the deacon asks the people to come forward to receive Communion: "With fear of God, faith and love, draw near!" Fear of God, faith, and love—these are the main criteria for our participation.

But the Liturgy does not end with Communion. Having received, we then give thanks. Indeed the very word *Eucharist* means thanksgiving. Thanksgiving sums up the very nature and purpose of the Liturgy and indeed of Christian life.

❧ 20 ❧

Thanksgiving and Dismissal

Then they told what happened on the way,
and how he was known to them in
the breaking of the bread.
—Lk. 24:35, vp

You may notice a change of atmosphere in the church after Holy Communion. There is a sense of fulfillment and joy. The intensity that had been building up until that point has been alleviated. The church somehow feels lighter. This joy is well expressed in the hymn that follows:

We have seen the true light! We have received the heavenly Spirit. We have found the true faith, as we worship the undivided Trinity. For the Trinity has saved us!

And the deacon again leads us in prayer:

20. *Bishop distributing the antidoron*

Stand upright. Having received the divine, holy, pure, immortal, heavenly, life-giving and dread Mysteries of Christ, let us give worthy thanks to the Lord.

And the clergy pray, saying:

We thank you, Lord, lover of mankind, benefactor of our souls, that you have counted us worthy today of your heavenly and immortal Mysteries. Make straight our way, establish us all in the fear of you, watch over our life, and make firm our steps, through the prayers and intercessions of the glorious Mother of God and Ever-Virgin Mary, and of all your Saints.

This is followed by what is called the Prayer Behind the Ambo, which the priest says in the middle of the church or before the icon of Christ on the icon screen:

·········▶ The word *ambo* comes from a Greek word meaning "an elevation." It was a raised platform, like an elaborate pulpit, in the middle of the nave from which the Epistle and Gospel would be read. In modern Eastern Orthodox Churches, it is very rare indeed. As a result, the Prayer Behind the Ambo is often read outside of the sanctuary before the icon screen.

O Lord, you bless those who bless you, and sanctify those who have put their trust in you: save your people and bless your inheritance; protect the fullness of your Church; sanctify those who love the beauty of your house; glorify them in return by your divine power, and do not forsake us who hope in you. Give peace to your world, to your churches, to the priests, to our rulers, and to all your people. For every good gift and every perfect gift is from above, coming down from you the Father of lights; and to you we give glory, thanksgiving, and worship, Father, Son, and Holy Spirit, now and for ever, and to the ages of ages.

And the choir sings thrice, "Blessed be the name of the Lord, from this time forth and forever more." Then the priest says the *apolysis* ("dismissal"), commemorating the saints and dismissing the people.

▶ After the dismissal, the people go up to the priest to take from him a small piece of bread called the *antidoron*, which means, "instead of the gifts," because it is given to those who did not receive Communion (but it is widespread practice for Communicants to receive it too). It is considered blessed bread, because it is taken from the loaves left over from the service of the *Proskomidi*, or is otherwise blessed by the priest during the Liturgy.

We have completed our journey to God's Kingdom. We have received Christ Himself in Communion. We have been in God's presence, like Moses before God on Mount Sinai.

So what happens now? Are we simply to remain in the church, rejoicing in God's presence? Of course not. Although it is good for us to remain there, we are dismissed, we are sent back out into the world, bearing the light and joy of God's presence. I am talking about what some theologians have described as "the liturgy after the Liturgy" (liturgy meaning "the work of the people").

I have described the Liturgy as a journey to God's Kingdom, but it can also be compared to another journey: the journey of Christ's disciples to Emmaus recorded in St. Luke's Gospel. Toward the end of this Gospel, we read that just a couple of days after Christ's crucifixion, two of Jesus's disciples were walking from Jerusalem to a village called Emmaus, discussing the events of the past couple of days. Jesus, now risen from the dead, joined them on the road, but they did not recognize him. As they walked, He explained to them how all that had happened to Jesus had been predicted by the Prophets. Inspired by His exegesis of the Scriptures, they persuaded Jesus to stay at the village and eat with them. As they sat at the table, Jesus took bread, blessed it, broke it, and gave it to them. All of a sudden, He vanished, and they realized that it was

Jesus. They rushed back to Jerusalem to proclaim the good news that Jesus had risen from the dead.

This is the journey we take at every Divine Liturgy. We have heard God's word and we have seen Christ in the breaking of bread. What comes next? In the story of the road to Emmaus, after the disciples realize that they have seen Christ, they hurry back to Jerusalem to look for the Apostles to tell them. Having seen the risen Christ, their immediate reaction is to share their joy. We too can have that same desire. We should not see our Faith as something that is merely "individual." "You are the light of the world," says the Lord (Matt. 5:14, NIV). We are called to share with all people the joy of the risen Christ. But first we must acquire that joy. If Christ is the source of humanity's joy, and we who are dedicated to Him have no joy, then what hope is there for the rest of the world? As St. Seraphim of Sarov famously said: "Acquire inward peace and a thousand souls around you will find their salvation."[33]

Thus there can be no true "evangelization," no effective "mission" without the Liturgy. We cannot proclaim the joy of the Resurrection unless we have experienced that joy for ourselves. This is why in the Lenten Liturgy of the Presanctified Gifts, just before Communion, we chant, "Taste and see that the Lord is good," and at Easter, "Receive the body of Christ and taste of the immortal spring." The proof of the pudding is in the eating. Taste, and then you will see.

When the first Apostles met Christ and asked where he was staying, the Lord replied, "Come and see." When Philip told Nathaniel that he has found the Messiah, and Nathaniel expressed his doubts, Philip said, "Come and see" (John 1:35–52). This invitation the Orthodox Church extends to all the world: "Come and see." If you want to learn about the Church, come to the Divine Liturgy and see for yourself.

Having seen for ourselves, we are sent out into the world that we may carry some of that light and joy of the Divine Liturgy with us. As we leave the church we are full of peace and gladness. When others see us leave the church, they may wonder what it is we have that they do not.

Ask yourself for a moment: What would happen if I, who have experienced God's presence, who have been touched by the radiant light of the risen Christ, were to transmit this spiritual joy to just one other person? If my faith quietly and subtly filled with peace and gladness everything I do and say? We would begin, slowly but surely, to change the world around us.

Only when we truly experience Christ in the Liturgy—when we not only hear of His sacrifice for humankind but also when we celebrate that sacrifice, when we receive Him into our very bodies in Holy Communion, making Him physically one with us, and thus be able to proclaim with the disciples, "We have seen the Lord! He spoke to us! He ate with us! We have touched Him! We have felt Him! He is alive! He is risen!"—only then can we truly be bearers of "the good news"; only then can we be "the light of the world."

The Church invites us all to enter into God's Kingdom, and to become, as far as possible, the Kingdom of Heaven on earth: "And the Spirit and the bride say, 'Come!' And let him who hears say, 'Come!' And let him who thirsts come. Whoever desires, let him take the water of life freely. . . . Even so, come, Lord Jesus!" (Rev. 22:17, 20, NKJV).

The Church of the Resurrection or a Church of Death?

P raying for the dead is a regular feature of Orthodox life. The most popular form of such prayer is the Memorial Service for the Departed, and in many places this service is regularly integrated into the Divine Liturgy.

The Memorial Service is a short service for one or a few specific people, since memorial services are held at particular times after a person's passing: on the third, sixth, ninth, and fortieth days after a person's passing away, then on the third, sixth, and ninth months, and then annual commemorations are held, as well as on the Saturdays set aside for the dead during the ecclesiastical year: the Saturdays of Souls. Memorial services should not be held from the Saturday of Lazarus (the day before Palm Sunday) until Thomas Sunday (the Sunday after Easter Sunday); nor on the holy days between Christmas and Theophany, at Pentecost, on all Holy Days of our Lord, and on the Dormition of the Mother of God. Furthermore, memorial services, according to Orthodox Tradition, are not to be held on Sundays. For Sunday is the day of the Resurrection—a mini Easter—and we are not to mourn death on this day. But because many people are either unwilling or unable to come to church at any other time, memorial services are commonly held on most Sundays of the year.

It is, however, most unfortunate that memorial services have become a regular feature of the Eucharistic assembly. For instead of leaving the church on a high—rejoicing as did the disciples on the road from Emmaus—we leave the church as though we have just been to a funeral.

In some places, memorial services on Sundays are held after the Liturgy as a completely separate service—following the Dismissal and distribution of the *antidoron*—solely for the family and friends of the departed. I am of two minds about this practice. On the one hand, it is preferable to adding it to the Divine Liturgy, so that those who are in church for the Liturgy may enjoy the service as it is; but on the other, it reduces memorial services to a private, family affair. The Church *is* the family, and all members of the Church should pray for one another, whether they are blood relations or not.

But why do we pray for the dead? We pray for the dead for two reasons: (1) We love them; (2) Christ has destroyed the power of death. Therefore, death cannot separate us from His Body, the Church. As Saint Paul writes: "I am convinced that neither death nor life, neither angels nor demons, neither the present nor the future, nor any powers, neither height nor depth, nor anything else in all creation, will be able to separate us from the love of God that is in Christ Jesus our Lord" (Rom. 8:38–39, NIV).

The center and fulfillment of all of the services and prayers of the Church, including those for the dead, is the Divine Liturgy. At the Holy Altar, all members of the Church, living and departed—present, past, and future— are "remembered" by God, even when we forget them. In St. Basil's Liturgy, the priest says:

> And those whom we have not remembered, through ignorance or forgetfulness or the number of the names, do you yourself remember, O God, who know the age and appellation of each, who know each from their mother's womb.

Memorial services need not be added to the Divine Liturgy, for Christ is with us in the Eucharist. "How can the guests of the bridegroom mourn while he is with them?" (Matt. 9:15, NIV). What more is there to be said or done? "For God is with us" (Isa. 8:10, NIV).

Acknowledgments

The English translations of the hymns and prayers of the Liturgy of St. John Chrysostom employed in this book are taken from the second edition of *The Divine Liturgy of Our Father Among the Saints John Chrysostom* of the Greek Orthodox Archdiocese of Thyateira and Great Britain (2011) by Fr. Ephrem Lash, while the prayers of St. Basil's Liturgy are taken from *The Divine Liturgy of Our Father Among the Saints Basil the Great* (Manchester, 2007) by the same translator.

The map of the Liturgy was designed by Mark Angel. All photographs are by Mark Angel and Iliana Giannousi (printed here by kind permission.)

I am also grateful to Fr. John Nankivell and Jon M. Sweeney for their assistance and suggestions.

Notes

1. In normal Greek practice, the Liturgy begins usually after the Matins service; in the Russian, usually after the service of the Hours.

2. Alexander Schmemann, *For the Life of the World* (Crestwood, NY: St. Vladimir's Seminary Press, 1973), 29–30.

3. Romano Guardini, *The Church and the Catholic, and the Spirit of the Liturgy* (New York: Sheed and Ward, 1950), 180–81.

4. Schmemann, *For the Life of the World*, 30.

5. Ephrem Lash, "A Simple Commentary on the Divine Liturgy," St. Anthony the Great and St. John the Baptist, Ecumenical Patriarchate of Constantinople and New Rome Archdiocese of Thyateira and Great Britain, http://orthodox-islington.org.uk/category/divine-liturgy, accessed May 1, 2012.

6. St. Germanus of Constantinople, *On the Divine Liturgy*, ed. Paul Meyendorff (Crestwood, NY: St. Vladimir's Seminary Press, 1985), 56.

7. Ignatius of Antioch, *To the Smyrneans* 8.1 and 2 (*The Apostolic Fathers*, vol. 1, ed. and trans. Bart D. Ehrman, Loeb Classical Library [Cambridge, MA: Harvard University Press, 2003]).

8. Alexander Schmemann, *The Eucharist* (Crestwood, NY: St. Vladimir's Seminary Press, 2000), 95.

9. Ibid, 96.

10. Ibid.

11. John Hainsworth, *The Ever-Virginity of the Mother of God*, as quoted at http://www.goarch.org/ourfaith/ourfaith9174, accessed May 1, 2012.

12. The Ever Virginity of the Mother of God, Fr. John Hainsworth, http://www.archdiocese.ca/e_resources/articles /JohnHainsworth.Ever_Virginity.pdf, accessed May 1, 2012.

13. Athanasius, *On the Incarnation* 54.3 (Migne, *Patrologia Graeca* 25, 192 B: De Incarnatione Verbi, 54).

14. Schmemann, *For the Life of the World*, 31–32.

15. John Chrysostom, *Homily on the Acts of the Apostles* 19.5, altered from http://blog.westsrbdio.org/2011/01/21 /the-meaning-of-our-divine-services-part-nine-divine-liturgy -%E2%80%9Cthe-thrice-holy-hymn%E2%80%9D/, accessed May 1, 2012.

16. Ephrem Lash, "A Simple Commentary on the Divine Liturgy."

17. Justin Martyr, *First Apology* 15.6, trans. Marcus Dods and George Reith, in *Ante-Nicene Fathers*, vol. 1, ed. Alexander Roberts, James Donaldson, and A. Cleveland Coxe (Buffalo, NY: Christian Literature Publishing Co., 1885). Revised and edited for New Advent by Kevin Knight, http://www.newadvent.org/fathers/0126.htm, accessed May 1, 2012.

18. John Chrysostom, *Ad Neophytos* (AD 388), trans. John Salza, http://www.scripturecatholic.com/baptism.html, accessed May 1, 2012.

19. St. John Chrysostom, *On the Incomprehensible Nature of God*, trans. Paul W. Harkins (Washington, DC: Catholic University of America Press, 1984), 106.

20. Ephrem Lash, "A Simple Commentary on the Divine Liturgy."

21. The book of the Orthodox Old Testament called 2 Kingdoms is known as 2 Kings in the Roman Catholic Old Testament (The Vulgate) and as 2 Samuel in the Protestant Old Testament.

22. Alexander Schmemann, *Great Lent: Journey to Pascha* (Crestwood, NY: St. Vladimir's Seminary Press, 2003), 126.

23. St. John Chrysostom, *Homily on 2 Corinthians* 18.13. Quoted in Schmemann, *Great Lent,* 117.

24. St. John Cassian, *Third Conference of Abbot Theonas on Sinlessness* 21. Quoted in Schmemann, *Great Lent,* 116.

25. Vladimir Lossky, *The Mystical Theology of the Eastern Church* (Crestwood, NY: St. Vladimir's Seminary Press, 1998), 15.

26. St. Maximus the Confessor, *On the Divine Names,* trans. Fr. Andrew Louth, in *Wisdom of the Greek Fathers* (Tring, Herts, UK: Lion, 1998), 1.4, p. 4, 208.

27. C. S. Lewis, *Mere Christianity* (New York: HarperCollins, 2002), 134.

28. Ephrem Lash, "A Simple Commentary on the Divine Liturgy."

29. St. John Chrysostom, *Homily on Matthew* 50.3–4 (PG 58:508–9).

30. Phyllis McGinley, *Saint-Watching* (New York: Viking, 1969), 5–6.

31. Lewis, *Mere Christianity,* 226.

32. Quoted in Timothy Ware, *The Orthodox Church* (New York: Penguin, 1997), 243.

33. Quoted in Archimandrite Lazarus Moore, *St Seraphim of Sarov: A Spiritual Biography* (Blanco, TX: New Sarov Press, 1994), 126.

ABOUT PARACLETE PRESS

WHO WE ARE

As the publishing arm of the Community of Jesus, Paraclete Press presents a full expression of Christian belief and practice—from Catholic to Evangelical, from Protestant to Orthodox, reflecting the ecumenical charism of the Community and its dedication to sacred music, the fine arts, and the written word. We publish books, recordings, sheet music, and video/DVDs that nourish the vibrant life of the church and its people.

WHAT WE ARE DOING

Books   PARACLETE PRESS BOOKS show the richness and depth of what it means to be Christian. While Benedictine spirituality is at the heart of who we are and all that we do, our books reflect the Christian experience across many cultures, time periods, and houses of worship.

We have many series, including *Paraclete Essentials*; *Paraclete Fiction*; *Paraclete Poetry*; *Paraclete Giants*; and for children and adults, *All God's Creatures*, books about animals and faith; and *San Damiano Books*, focusing on Franciscan spirituality. Others include *Voices from the Monastery* (men and women monastics writing about living a spiritual life today), *Active Prayer*, and new for young readers: *The Pope's Cat*. We also specialize in gift books for children on the occasions of Baptism and First Communion, as well as other important times in a child's life, and books that bring creativity and liveliness to any adult spiritual life.

The Mount Tabor Books series focuses on the arts and literature as well as liturgical worship and spirituality; it was created in conjunction with the Mount Tabor Ecumenical Centre for Art and Spirituality in Barga, Italy.

Music   THE PARACLETE RECORDINGS label represents the internationally acclaimed choir *Gloriæ Dei Cantores*, the *Gloriæ Dei Cantores Schola*, and the other instrumental artists of the *Arts Empowering Life Foundation*.

Paraclete Press is the exclusive North American distributor for the Gregorian chant recordings from St. Peter's Abbey in Solesmes, France. Paraclete also carries all of the Solesmes chant publications for Mass and the Divine Office, as well as their academic research publications.

In addition, PARACLETE PRESS SHEET MUSIC publishes the work of today's finest composers of sacred choral music, annually reviewing over 1,000 works and releasing between 40 and 60 works for both choir and organ.

Video   Our video/DVDs offer spiritual help, healing, and biblical guidance for a broad range of life issues including grief and loss, marriage, forgiveness, facing death, understanding suicide, bullying, addictions, Alzheimer's, and Christian formation.

Learn more about us at our website:
www.paracletepress.com, or
call us toll-free at 1-800-451-5006.

SCAN
TO
READ
MORE

You may also be interested in ...

The Grace of Incorruption
**The Selected Essays of Donald Sheehan
on Orthodox Faith and Poetics**
Donald Sheehan,
Edited by Xenia Sheehan,
Foreword by Christopher Merrill

ISBN 978-1-61261-601-8 | $26.99

Giver of Life
The Holy Spirit in Orthodox Tradition
Fr. John W. Oliver

ISBN 978-1-55725-675-1 | $18.99

Available at bookstores
Paraclete Press | 1-800-451-5006
www.paracletepress.com

CPSIA information can be obtained
at www.ICGtesting.com
Printed in the USA
BVHW081622021219
565404BV00003B/463/P